NUMBER ONE!

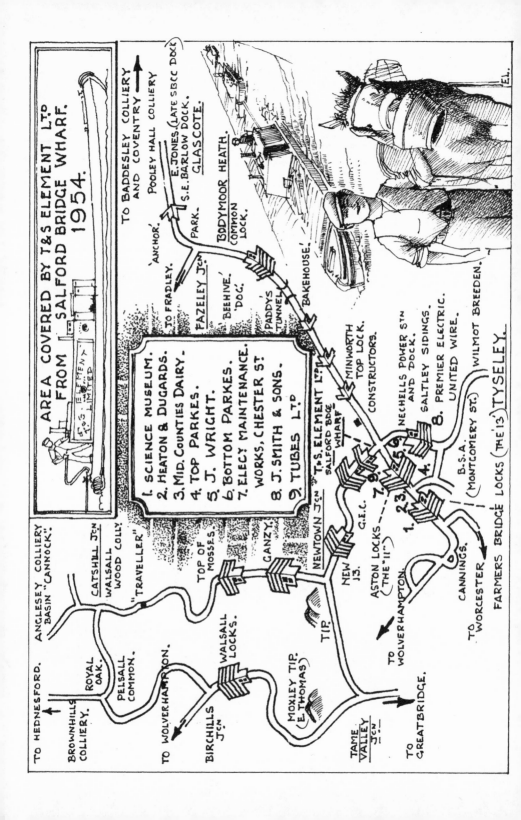

AREA COVERED BY T&S ELEMENT Lᵀᴰ
FROM SALFORD BRIDGE WHARF.
1954.

T.S. ELEMENT
LIMITED

1. SCIENCE MUSEUM.
2. HEATON & DUGARDS.
3. MID. COUNTIES DAIRY.
4. TOP PARKES.
5. J. WRIGHT.
6. BOTTOM PARKES.
7. ELECᵞ MAINTENANCE.
   WORKS, CHESTER Sᵀ
8. J. SMITH & SONS.
9. TUBES Lᵀᴰ

TO BADDESLEY COLLIERY AND COVENTRY.
POOLEY HALL COLLIERY.
E. JONES (LATE SBCC DOCK)
S.E. BARLOW DOCK.
GLASCOTE.

'ANCHOR'.
TO FRADLEY.
PARK.
FAZELEY JCⁿ
BODYMOOR HEATH.
COMMON LOCK.
'BEEHIVE'. 'DOG'.
PADDYS TUNNEL.
'BAKEHOUSE'.
MINWORTH TOP LOCK.
CONSTRUCTORS.
G.E.C.
NEWTOWN JCⁿ
T&S ELEMENT Lᵀᴰᵖ
SALFORD BDGE WHARF.
7. 9. 6. 5.
CANZY.
TOP OF MOSSES.
1. 2. 3. 4.
NECHELLS POWER Sᵀⁿ AND DOCK.
SALTLEY SIDINGS.
8. PREMIER ELECTRIC.
UNITED WIRE.
B.S.A. WILMOT BREEDEN.
(MONTGOMERY Sᵀ.)
TYSELEY.
CANNINGS.
TO WORCESTER.
FARMERS BRIDGE LOCKS (THE '13')

ASTON LOCKS (THE '11')
NEW 13.
TO WOLVERHAMPTON.
TIP.

TO HEDNESFORD.
BROWNHILLS COLLIERY.
ANGLESEY COLLIERY
BASIN "CANNOCK".
CATSHILL JCⁿ
WALSALL WOOD COLLY.
"TRAVELLER"
ROYAL OAK.
PELSALL COMMON.
TO WOLVERHAMPTON.
BIRCHILLS JCⁿ
WALSALL LOCKS.
MOXLEY TIP. (E. THOMAS)
TAME VALLEY JCⁿ
TO GREATBRIDGE.

E.L.

Tom Foxon

NUMBER ONE !

Illustrations by Brian Collings

J. M. Pearson & Son
Burton-on-Trent

First impression 1991
by J.M. Pearson & Son (Publishers) Ltd.
Tatenhill Common
Burton-on-Trent
Staffordshire

British Library Cataloguing in Publication Data
Foxon, Tom
Number one.
I. Title
386.40424092

ISBN 0 907864 58 9

Printed by Penwell Print Limited of Callington, Cornwall

FOR JEANNE

CONTENTS

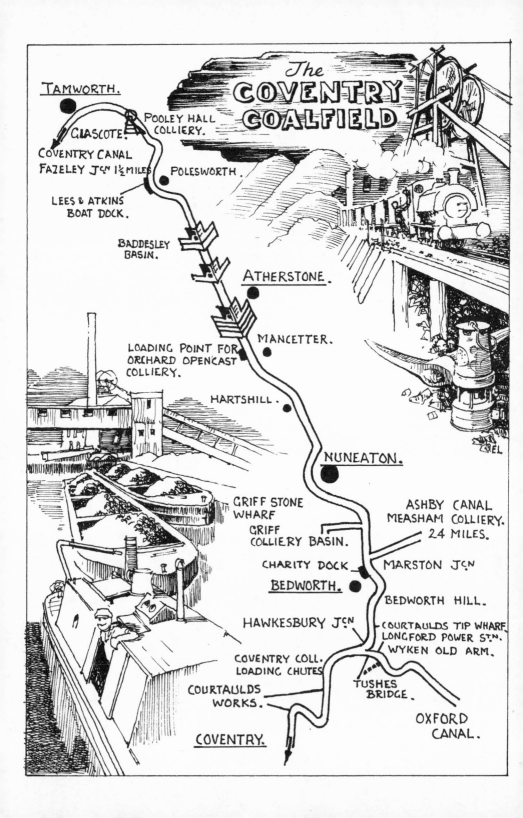

INTRODUCTION

"Babbyshit"

Thus spake Sooty Barrett, giving his considered opinion on the colour of my oak-grained paintwork.

There was a thud as the grab dropped into the hold of the S.E. Barlow motorboat which occupied the unloading length opposite us. The overhead conveyors rumbled, carrying a stream of coal above our heads into the power station. The hint of a summer breeze spread a fine powdering of black dust over everything in sight.

Reaching into the ticket drawer for a packet of Player's Weights, I lit one up and smiled innocently at Sooty. Now was the time, I thought, to try and trap him in one of those question and answer routines which were popular among the youth of the day. The object was to get the unwary victim to answer 'Who?', 'What?' or 'Where?'; thus laying himself open to a vulgar retort.

"Have you been down there lately?", I enquired in an off-hand manner.

Sooty fell for it.

"Where?", he asked...

This was Longford Power Station on the Oxford Canal in 1955. I drew in a lungfull of smoke, took a swallow of the tea which Sooty's brother Ken had just produced for us, and thought back to the train of events which had brought me here.

* * *

It had all begun some four years before when, at the age of sixteen, I had left my home and office job to work on 'The Cut'. The mate of a canal boat could lead a hard and insecure life in the course of learning his trade, and my own experiences had been no exception. But the prospect of eventually becoming a captain, and being given charge of one of the British Waterways motorboats operating between the Mersey and the Midlands, had prompted me to persevere. My goal had just been within my grasp when I was called up for National Service, the last two years of which were spent in Egypt.

Prior to call up I had been a mate on British Waterways boats in the North Western Division and, as the three year engagement put the same obligation on employers as did National Service – i.e. to re-employ staff who had been called up – I decided that my future career lay with them. By late 1953, with only a few months left to go, I was about to write to British Waterways informing them that I wanted to return to canal work, when a letter arrived from John Knill, who I had worked for when I first went boating. He had recently bought another motor boat but had decided to re-sell it and wanted to know if I was interested. A photograph was enclosed.

The boat was the *Hesperus*, a wooden motor built at Rickmansworth in 1936 for the Grand Union Canal Carrying Company. She had been sold out of service and bought by Lord Lucan who used her as a pleasure boat. John had intended to restore her to trading condition but his plans had fallen through. He wanted £150 and estimated that she needed a similar amount spent on her.

Hesperus had already had an adventurous career since Lord Lucan bought her from the Grand Union Canal Carrying Co. in 1947. She had navigated the entire length of the Kennet & Avon Canal in 1948, a journey beset with many difficulties, before braving the Severn estuary en route to Sharpness. From there she voyaged to Manchester before crossing England by the Trent & Mersey Canal, the River Trent, and the Fossdyke & Witham to Boston, where she made an exciting crossing of the Wash before rejoining the canal system via the River Nene.

It didn't take me long to make up my mind to buy *Hesperus* and to embark on the career of an owner-boatman, or 'Number One' as they were known in canal parlance. Time was when there had been many Number Ones on the canals, but cut-throat competition in the 1930s, particularly from the then newly formed GUCCCo, had decimated their ranks. When I started boating in 1950 only a handful remained.

Since the war the attitude of the larger carriers had changed. The private enterprise firms, who were mainly in the coal trade, now preferred to sub-contract any surplus traffic rather than enlarge their fleets. The commission charges, which varied but rarely exceeded 10%, were small but they represented certain profit, and the owner boatmen could easily be dispensed with if trade fell off. The nationalised sector, trying to cope with irregular shipment traffic of dubious profitability, were equally glad to sub-contract. One traffic officer in the North West, was heard to express the view that he would like to turn over the whole carrying operation to private enterprise and just collect tolls. In such circumstances there was plenty of opportunity for a Number One to make a living; particularly as his overheads were reduced by the use of his boat as a dwelling. Several small carriers started up in the immediate post-war period but, employing boatmen in a difficult labour market, soon went to the wall, whereas as owner/boatmen they could have flourished.

It was John Knill who saw that, in order to get new traffics on the canal, it would be necessary to combine the low costs of small carriers with a central organisation for obtaining traffic. Unfortunately this scheme never got off the ground but, at the time, it was anticipated that I should take part, together with his brother-in-law, who also intended to have a pair of boats. The idea of sub-contracting, rather than being tied down to contracts of my own, appealed to my romantic nature as offering the opportunity to roam over the canal system "following the trade."

Like many another young boatman, I was thoroughly steeped in boating tradition. My vision of life in the future was of a spotlessly clean, brightly painted boat, agleam with polished brass and scrubbed woodwork, working briskly over the Midland waterways system. I would rise early, tie up late, and as I intended to make a name for myself, often work all night! Just how far my dreams were to be translated into reality will be related. Meanwhile, having paid for *Hesperus* and arranged for John to start the necessary work on her, I waited with mounting impatience for demob.

Chapter One

NEW HOPE

T ime passes slowly when you are young and the last months of my service seemed never-ending. When at long last the orders for my return
to England were posted, life assumed a dreamlike quality. After so long in
the Zone, our small group found it hard to believe that we were actually
going home, and we dreaded the possibility that some last minute emer-
gency might occur to extend our service. Even when we were finally seated
aboard a Hermes aircraft, winging through the night towards England,
this air of unreality persisted.

After a stop for refuelling at Luqa in Malta, where we were given tea and
sandwiches, we took off again. Too excited to sleep, we conversed quietly
as the aircraft droned through the night, to decant us at about 5 a.m. into
the cold, clammy darkness of an April morning in Blackbushe. Then
began the tiresome rigmarole inseparable from demob, which was to
occupy three more days. Our party was transported to Hendon to be fed
and watered before being despatched to RAF Innsworth at Gloucester.
This part of the journey took place by train and fellow ex-servicemen will
share my recollections of the ordeal of travelling with full kit on the crowded Underground.

Comfortably settled at last on a westbound express, its 'Castle' class
engine eating up the miles through the Thames Valley and over the
Cotswolds, reality returned and we began to make excited plans for our
first few days at home. An English April can be exceedingly inclement, but
for us the weather was as kind as the two nurses that a friend and I
encountered in Gloucester that evening, for it was warm enough to sit out
in the park and enjoy their company; our first female society for two years.

The formalities at Innsworth dragged on and on, and there were
attempts to enforce Service discipline right up to the end. But eventually
the final stamp descended on the last document and I was a civilian again;
albeit still in uniform, as the Forces parting shot was to make us travel all

the way to Woking in order to collect our demob suits. Instead of proceeding there directly, I went first to visit my girlfriend in Bristol, travelling from there to Woking which, conveniently, was on the way to Southsea where my parents lived.

Free at last, and with money in my pocket, I relaxed for a few days. England, it seemed, had changed little in my absence. Gone alas were the trams in London and Birmingham; a city without trams being, to me, like an egg without salt. But the railway system was little altered, and the familiar friends of my childhood still raced along the main lines or ambled along some rural byway, wreathed in steam and accompanied by the clatter of wheels. I could see that the countryside was as I had always known it, a land of small fields, hedges, woodland, flowery meadows, ponds and streams. For one all too brief period England was poised between the end of the poverty of the Thirties, the hardships of war, and the impending onslaught of the consumer society. It was a time to be savoured, a fleeting Golden Age. Within little more than a decade the last steam locomotive would disappear and only a handful of canal boats remain in trade, while hideous motorways would be carved through some of our most beautiful and precious countryside, cities ripped apart and whole urban communities destroyed to accommodate the car and the juggernaut lorry.

Fortunately, in those early April days of 1954 the vision of the future was mercifully withheld. England seemed unchanged and unchangeable, and I had my part to play in the pageant of beauty and tradition. In a small canalside village, hidden away in the Midlands, *Hesperus* was waiting.

It was time to be gone.

* * *

I had written to John Knill to let him know of my return to England and had received a reply advising me to travel north by the Great Central line. Thus it was, that having reached London by Southern Electric and crossed it by the Bakerloo Line, I presented myself at Marylebone station.

To me a great railway station was reminiscent of a cathedral; not just in its imposing architecture, but as the setting for an unchanging ritual celebrated time after time for many years. All eyes would be on the clock as the minute hand approached departure time. The platform inspector operated the 'train ready to start' plunger, alerting the signalman who, standing before his array of shining levers and instruments, beat out a code on the block bell to 'ask the road' from the box in advance, watching for his instrument to indicate 'line clear' so that he could clear the departure signal. On the platform, to the accompaniment of shrieking whistles and slamming doors, the guard would hold up his green flag, while the fireman pronounced the time-honoured words 'right away!' and the driver heaved open the regulator handle. Slowly, but with ever increasing speed, the train would gather way, the guard stepping nonchalantly aboard his moving brake-van. The first loud blasts of the exhaust would diminish as the signalman sent the two beats of 'train entering section' signal forward and stood at his window to observe the tail lamp.

There was a long established departure from Marylebone to the North at 3.20 p.m., and I was there in good time to walk up the platform and watch our engine being coupled on. A few years previously we would have had a 'Director' or 'Sandringham' locomotive, but now we had a huge, grimy Gresley 'Pacific', named *Hyperion*. The train was very lightly patronised and I enjoyed a compartment to myself. This was the first time that I had travelled on this line, and from my comfortable seat I was able to relax and enjoy the scenery. The long climb over the Chilterns culminated in our first stop at Aylesbury, and as soon as we got away from there the countryside assumed the unmistakeable ambience of the Midlands, and I experienced a great sense of coming home. I alighted at Woodford, having time for a cup of tea in the refreshment room before the arrival of the connecting local. Woodford was the epitome of an English country junction of the period, places to be remembered with affection, especially when encountered on such a happy and hopeful journey as this.

The local train rattled in and soon we were in the heart of the Northamptonshire Uplands. Stopping briefly at Charwelton, we plunged into Catesby Tunnel, emerging to drop down into the valley of the Leam. I had a glimpse of the canal as we crossed it at Wolfhampcote, and then we were running into Braunston & Willoughby station. John Knill was waiting for me on the platform, from which we descended by a flight of steps to the road where his car awaited. A mile down the road we crossed the canal and turned left, negotiating the long village street and emerging on to a narrow field track which led to the old farm house at the top lock, from where he ran his pairs of boats.

After breakfast the next morning, John and I walked down the locks. He had rented the wharf and shed by the bottom lock and employed an old boatbuilder, compulsorily retired from Barlows, to do odd jobs. Tied up alongside was *Hesperus*.

The previous evening John had confessed that, having omitted to drain the engine in the winter, the cylinder block had frozen and cracked. This was repairable by welding which he would pay for, so I was not particularly worried, although there was some delay in finding somebody who could weld cast iron and the boat had to be towed to Tamworth for the job to be done.

Examining the boat carefully, I was disturbed to find that both top bends were badly cracked, something that had not been revealed to me in our correspondence prior to purchase. It was commonly supposed that because of the large order, boats built at Rickmansworth for the G.U.C.C.Co. contained unseasoned timber, and John attributed the cracks to 'green wood'. As I later discovered the iron stem bar to be loose, I am now inclined to think that the problem may have been caused by collision damage. Such a major fault really merited a reduction in purchase price, but lacking as I was in business experience, it never occurred to me to ask for one. Although the boat's value was diminished, it didn't really affect its working ability, as the cracks were above the loaded water line. I puttied them up and eventually had them plated over at Worsey's dock, who made such a good job of it that you had to look very closely to see the repair.

I was also surprised to find that the work which had already been done on my behalf included a complete new set of false floors in the hold, a very expensive job. She also had new top planks, stretchers, uprights, deckboard, false cratch and cratch boards. The mast and beams were second-hand. There were no side or top cloths. All the paintwork had been given a coat of priming inside and out.

The next few weeks were occupied by the satisfying routine of preparing the boat, which I had decided to rename *New Hope*, for her return to carrying. The days passed pleasantly and the Knills were hospitable and entertaining company. In the soft April evenings I would sometimes enjoy a solitary stroll, often over the old horse path above the tunnel, soaking in the atmosphere of the English countryside of which I had for so long been deprived. On other occasions I was enlisted to escort the Knills' glamourous Swiss au-pair to the local youth club for an orgy of table tennis and coffee. Once or twice I went to Daventry with John to attend the somewhat duller meetings of the Chamber of Commerce.

The cabin was the first thing to attend to on *New Hope*. This I oak-grained in the traditional manner, picking out the mouldings in red and green. The insides of the cupboards were painted light blue as was the custom. When this was completed and varnished, I set about buying the necessary 'cabin things'. Cooking and eating utensils came from the village store, but I had to go to Daventry for the spring mattress. This was my one departure from tradition – boatmen used flock beds. During the day, bedding was stored in the bed cupboard, and it was always a struggle to persuade my bulky mattress into this confined space. Also from Daventry came a Primus stove, something few boatmen would be without.

Now that the cabin was habitable I moved in. As yet it lacked any decorative touches in the way of curtains, brasses and hanging up plates, but these would come in the fullness of time. The range had come out of John's butty *Uranus* and was of the enamelled variety with a cast iron top which I religiously black-leaded.

Half a mile down the cut was the dockyard of the Samuel Barlow Coal Co. When I had worked on their boats for a while in 1950, Frank Nurser had been the manager, but he had retired and the new manager was a Mr Le Cheminant, known to the boatmen as 'Lee Shan'. He was not very popular, having sacked several boatmen for such time-honoured diversions as fighting on the dock. One unfortunate boatman, whose headlamp had failed, ventured into Braunston tunnel lit only by a candle in a jam jar, and had been sacked for colliding with another boat. My only encounter with Le Cheminant was to order a cabin chimney, for which I was charged the then outrageous sum of two pounds and ten shillings.

John Knill and I spent a lot of time discussing the canal carrying trade. Back in 1954 there was still a body of opinion which held that trade could be won back to the canal. John himself had a new contract carrying coal to the Colne Valley Sewage works and had also regained the carriage of domestic coal to Banbury Co-op. Now and again he obtained back cargoes from London which were new to the canal. Unfortunately the salt contract to Reading and Newbury, on which I had worked in 1950, had reverted to rail amid dark mutterings that the consignees had been 'got at'. While I had been in Egypt a new carrying firm, the Wyvern Shipping Co. of Leighton Buzzard, had started trading using the famous motor boat *Heatherbell* and several boats from the now defunct firm of John Green of Macclesfield. John Knill's brother-in-law was preparing a pair of boats to trade as the Coronet Canal Carrying Co., while rumours abounded about the bright new star that was about to rise on the horizon, the Willow Wren Canal Carrying Co.

One day, while walking up the locks to have my lunch at the Knills, I encountered the first Willow Wren pair, *Warbler* and *Wagtail*, captained by Sam Horne, and looking a picture in their bright new paintwork, polished brass, and scrubbed white strings and woodwork. This caused great excitement at the top lock as we speculated what the new firm might be likely to carry.

It had been more or less agreed that John would organise the traffic for both myself and his brother-in-law. With this in mind we had agreed on a rate of 12/6d ton from Baddesley Colliery to Banbury Co-op inclusive of unloading by means of shovel and barrow. An average load of 23 tons would bring in £14.3s.6d and would take about six days including loading and discharging. Fuel costs would be 30/- per trip and, allowing for the fortnight of colliery holidays, the canal being closed by ice, and delays from other causes, one might expect to do 45 trips per year earning about £540.

It was thought provident to set aside £100 a year for boat maintenance, so I would be left with an income of about £9 per week. At the time, a boatmen employed by one of the established carrying companies might have expected to average £6.10/- a week on this particular job. One item of costing which we did not tackle was the cost of replacing a boat. Given the long life of a canal boat (Charlie Ballinger's *Thomas* worked for 48 years) John and I probably assumed that this was a calculation of no great importance.

As it had been arranged that the engine should be repaired at Glascote, where the 'Limited' dock had been taken over by an ex sea-going engineer, Ted Jones, I also decided to have *New Hope* caulked, tarred and the cabinside lettering done at the adjacent Anchor Dock of S.E. Barlow. So, one afternoon, I hooked on behind John Knill's *Kenelm* and *Uranus*, captained by Ron Wilson, to be towed to Tamworth, arriving there the following day. I had decided that, as it would not be very comfortable living aboard whilst perched up on top of the slipway, I would do a trip with my old friend Ray White, now captain of a Ballinger horse boat trading on the Worcester & Birmingham Canal, while the work was being done. As soon as I had seen *New Hope* winched out of the water, jacked up, and dropped on her blocks, and having had a good look below the water line and being pleased to find no discernable wear on the bottoms and bottom strake, I headed for the station and set off for Tardebigge.

CHAPTER TWO

HORSE BOAT INTERLUDE

Alighting from the train at Bromsgrove, I followed a country lane for one and a half miles, to find myself on a hump-backed bridge crossing the Worcester & Birmingham Canal below the 18th lock of the Tardebigge flight. Locks stretched in both directions as far as the eye could see. Examining them, I could see that all of the chambers were empty, which indicated that no uphill boat had recently passed. So I set off downhill; being not far from the bottom of the flight of thirty locks when *Thomas* came into sight.

Ray's mate Muriel gave me a quick cup of tea as *Thomas* rose in the lock, I undertook to 'drive and draw'. In the days when I had been a mate on the Shropshire Union route, where butties were hauled by horses through the flights at Audlem and Wolverhampton, I had become used to working with horses and soon fell into the old routine. At the tail of each lock I had to slack the horse so as to throw the tow-line over the bottom gate. As the boat entered the chamber, and approached its top end, the cry of "Draw!" would ring out, and I would whip up a paddle which would admit a flow of water to stop the boat from striking the upper cill. The boat would then have to be tied up tight against the top gate. If it was allowed to drift back the massive wooden rudder, or 'elum', might be caught between the closing bottom gates and reduced to matchwood. Then I drew the ground paddle on the other side of the lock, followed by the centre, or gate paddle. Meanwhile, Ray, having skilfully steered the unwieldy craft up the short pound and lined it up straight to enter the lock (a 'cross-wind' might result in a broken plank) had run up the offside steps with a short shaft. With this he pushed against the opposite gate, at the same time closing the one on his side of the lock. The massive timber fabrications would creak out from their recesses in the lock wall and, as the incoming water got behind them, would close with a satisfying thud. The time taken to fill the lock could be measured in seconds, soon the horse would be leaning into his collar and we would be straining against the balance beam of the top gate, to get it open as soon as possible. Then it was "Gee-up!", and Ray would leap aboard the swiftly accelerating boat, insert the tiller and line *Thomas* up for the next lock.

We tied up at Tardebigge New Wharf, making the horse comfortable for the night in his stable, and ordering the tunnel tug for the morning. This tug would tow *Thomas* all the way to Kings Norton through the tunnels at Tardebigge, Shortwood and Wast Hill, the last being over a mile long. It was in the stygian depths of Wast Hill tunnel that I once saw the exhaust funnel of a tug catch fire, an awe-inspiring sight in the pitch dark cavern. "Putting the fire up the pipe," was an expression commonly used by boatmen to describe hard driving, but this was the only occasion when I saw it translated into reality.

It was a pleasant task to lead the horse over the bracken fringed (and reputedly adder-haunted) paths which traversed the tops of the tunnels. Between the tunnels the horse followed the boat along the towpath of his own accord. At the east end of Wast Hill the tug cast us off. Bob was 'pegged to' to pull us at a sedate pace into Birmingham, where we tied up at Worcester Bar lock.

The next day saw us setting off into the intricate maze of waterways that led to the Cannock Chase Colliery wharf at Anglesey Basin, a fascinating journey in those far off days. Except between Smethwick and Spon Lane, where it ran in a deep cutting, the canalside was lined with busy industry all the way from Birmingham to Wednesbury. Junctions and side basins abounded. Here we would look into the clamorous heart of a rolling mill as a gang of men man-handled a long strip of red hot metal with their tongs, there we would glimpse the shape of a boat in some gloomy hole where an arm of the canal ran into a factory, and see the flash of shovels as her black cargo was fed into the furnaces. At night the street lamps shone like stars on the distant ridge above Dudley, and the darkness would be riven by skyward-leaping flames as the blast furnace cones at Bilston were lowered to admit a charge.

Every now and then we would meet a boat: perhaps a British Waterways motor with a cargo of dates for HP Sauce, or an empty Thomas Clayton heading for the great gasworks complexes of Windsor Street or Nechells to collect its pleasant smelling load of tar. But most numerous were the coal boats, their horses plodding steadily along the towpath, the water chuckling as it was parted by their bluff bows as they made their unobtrusive way to power station, factory or wharf. The very life blood of midlands industry was on the move, yet so secretive was the canal, so remote from the outside world, that few people were aware that over a million tons a year of cargo were carried on Birmingham's waterway.

After some seven hours of twisting and turning through this complicated network, we found ourselves proceeding up a narrow channel with the gaunt shape of the Cannock Chase colliery loading apparatus in front of us. Boats lined the canal on both sides as we pulled and shafted our way towards the loading chute. Waiting for an Ernest Thomas tug to finish assembling its tow of five boats for Birchills power station, we winded with some difficulty in the confined space.

Normally we would have loaded and gone back the short distance to tie up for the night at the "Traveller's Rest" at Walsall Wood. But, most unusually, for loading was normally very quick at 'Cannock', there was none of our grade of coal in any of the wagons that had come down from the pit head before knocking-off time. So we put the horse in the stable, had a meal, and then went for a walk around the huge reservoir of Chasewater which supplies the canal at this point.

When darkness fell, Anglesey Basin, to give it its proper name, became a romantic place. Above us loomed the mysterious tangle of ironwork which constituted the loading apparatus. The surrounding boats were shadowy shapes, their mooring chains creaking occasionally, while every now and then we would hear the plop of a water rat and see the V shaped ripples as it swam across the canal. The pit head was out of sight. There were no houses nearby, and the night was very quiet. Many years before, the mine workings had been right against the canal, and parts of the area were lit by an eerie blue glow where the subterranean gases still seeped to the surface and ignited.

In the morning, I was able to study the method of working. The coal came down from the pit head by mineral railway, each wagon being upended by a rotary tippler on to a conveyor belt which carried it up to the loading gantry spanning the arm. There were two chutes, one for loading large coal which could not be dropped into a boat from a great height, the other for smaller sizes. There were aquatic shunters – known as 'boat-snappers' – who, according to the grade of coal that was running, would select a boat from among those waiting and place it under the chute for loading. They needed to know which boats required which sort of coal, and, out of those, which one was likely to be collected by tug or horse first. In the Joey boat system of working, whereby boats were exchanged at the end of each journey, those left to await loading or discharge were known as 'standed' boats, and part of the art of a Joey boat operator was to maximise his return from capital and labour by ensuring that the optimum number of 'standed' boats were provided.

The 'boat-snappers' would know, for example, that all the Stewart's & Lloyds boats needed to be loaded with DS, or double-screened, nuts and at what time their daily tug would arrive. Some carriers loading to more than one destination, like Leonard Leigh, would have a metal plate fixed to the cabin side to indicate this, for instance, "Weldless Steel Tubes". Firms like T & S Element, with a wide variety of less regular loads, would carry no indication on the boat and loading requirements would be phoned through on a daily basis.

The system was complicated by the haulage arrangements, for in this trade there was a distinction between the providers of boats and the providers of tugs, horses and crews. The latter were known as 'steerers'. You would see, for instance, Leonard Leigh tugs hauling boats of the Central Electricity Authority, while their own boats might be hauled by an Element's horse to Tyseley, or a Number One tug to Wednesfield.

In May 1954 the only cabin boats (ie where the crews lived on board) visiting Cannock were those of Charles Ballinger of Gloucester, owner of the *Thomas*. These loaded small coal for Townsend's mill at Worcester, and large coal for the steam dredgers on the River Severn and for the domestic supply of the Worcester & Birmingham lock-keepers. It was the practice, so far as possible, to give cabin boats priority, and on some occasions you could be in and out of the basin in half an hour. Obviously there were times when the amount of a particular size of coal was insufficient to fill a boat. In which case the vessel would be taken out of the length, and loading of other boats with other sizes would continue apace, until its particular type of coal started running again, when it would be returned to the length and loading completed. The whole system was extremely efficient, in marked contrast to that obtaining at most of the Warwickshire colliery loading places where you were lucky to get loaded the day after arrival.

Work had hardly started when *Thomas* was ordered into the loading length beneath the small coal chute. The chutes lay fore and aft in relation to the boat's hold, which meant that the stands had to be removed for loading, and it was not too easy to get the coal in front of the mast. The coal, a mixture of pea slack with a little DS, was washed, so there was a complete absence of the dust which was associated with so many loading and discharging operations. Removal of the stands, meant that the top planks could not be put up and secured on top of them, to form a gangway from the cabin to the fore-end, and they had to be laid on top of the coal. Boats going on to the River Severn had to have their side-cloths up to give them additional freeboard, and for these the stands were allowed to remain in position, although it made loading much slower.

As the coal poured into the boat, Ray told me to look over the side. I did so and found the water to be so clear that the bottom of the canal could be clearly seen, even to the extent of reading the labels on the baked bean tins thrown overboard by some untidy boatman. Ray piled the coal fairly high towards the rear of the hold, leaving the 'back of the mast' light, and putting a moderate heap in front of the mast. With old wooden boats it was always best to keep the middle light, as this tended to keep the bottoms tight and prevent leaking. With many boats, loading like this improved their steering qualities. The Joey boats were loaded in three heaps, one in the back-end, one across the middle-beam, and one in the fore-end. A clear space was kept between the fore and middle heaps. This was known as the 'lade-hole', and was for scooping out water and also so that the mast step was left clear because boatmen had to change their mast and other 'tools' over from the arriving empty boat to a departing loaded one.

We came out of the length with 27 tons on board and man-handled our-selves out of the throng of boats to a position where we could attach the horse. As he leaned into the collar, *Thomas* started to move and respond to the helm. There is nothing quite so pleasant as travelling on a horse-drawn narrowboat. Lacking adequate words of my own, I must quote that great lover of horse boats, L.T.C. Rolt: "It is motion asleep." It will be argued that there was nothing pleasant about it in adverse weather condi-tions, which is perfectly true, but the same can be said for motor-boating, and indeed for many outdoor jobs. When the weather was reasonable it was nice to be without the noise and vibration of an engine, and to escape the inevitable smell of diesel oil, to walk along the towpath with the horse or to feel the long, heavy boat respond to the tiller. There were other advantages too: with no propellor it was impossible to get the blades fouled with the wide variety of rubbish which littered the bottom of many canals, the removal of which was the most difficult and tiresome aspect of boating; and if you should happen to go aground, haulage from the bank was much more effective than a propellor, it always being possible to rig up your block rope so as to get a two to one purchase.

We had not gone far when we came to the end of the Anglesey Arm, at the top of the disused Ogley Locks, and turned right on to the main line of the Wyrley & Essington Canal, only to make a sharp turn to the left shortly after at Catshill Junction on to the Daw End Branch. This was an awkward turn because of the narrow stop-place at the entrance to the branch which required the boat to be carefully lined up. We were now in an area of mining subsidence, the banks having been built up over the years to leave the canal high above the surrounding countryside. Places like this were among the few on the narrow canal system where you had really deep water under the boat, despite the constant unloading of boat-loads of clay into the canal to bring the bottom up and prevent excessive water pressure on the banks.

As soon as we got through Catshill Stop the cabin chimney was taken off its collar and laid flat on the cabin top, the water can was removed and put in the hatches, and the telescopic mast – which is always raised when tow-ing a loaded boat – was lowered in its case so that only the looby projected. Before long the reason for these precautions came in sight, a railway bridge so low that it seemed that even our deeply loaded boat would never get under. Passing the loading basin for Walsall Wood Colliery on our left, where coal was being shovelled out of railway wagons into a Tyseley bound Leonard Leigh Joey boat, we approached this fearsome looking obstacle without slackening speed. The horse's legs disappeared from sight as he plunged into a deep trench cut into the towpath to give him headroom. Our tiller was thrust hard over for the inside bend under the bridge, and the steerer dropped down into the cabin, not to re-appear until we were safely through. Heavily rivetted steel girders skimmed by only inches above our cabin top. With chimney, can and mast restored to their usual posi-tions, the next obstacle to be negotiated was the main road bridge at Walsall Wood, situated in the middle of a sharp S bend, a test of skill for the helmsman at the best of times, but made more tricky by the inability to see oncoming traffic. As we had a crew of three I was able to go ahead and report 'all clear'.

On our right, between the main road and the towpath, lay the backyards of a row of terrace houses and a pub. This was the "Traveller's Rest", or 'Traveller', as it was more usually referred to, and while it goes largely unsung in books about canals, it was the last canalside pub where a group of horse boats would tie up and stable their horses for the night. A buxom woman carrying a baby appeared at the yard gate of one of the houses, and a shouted conversation – in broad Black Country dialect on her part – took place with Muriel over the ever widening gap between us.

However, it was only half past nine in the morning and we would not be stopping there this trip. Indeed 'The Traveller' disappeared from view almost immediately as we slid under another low bridge, round a sharp left-hand turn, and found ourselves running alongside the rather inaptly named Utopia Works of the Aldridge Brick, Tile & Coal Company. Here they made the famous Staffordshire Blue engineering bricks, a few of which were still loaded on to boats, mainly for the purpose of building up the canal walls in places of mining subsidence.

From here to Rushall village we sailed high above the sunken moonscape of exhausted mineral workings, nowadays much built over, but then quite open and typical of Black Country wasteland, a mixture of hillocks, scrub and flashes or pools caused by subsidence. It always seemed to be windy up here, making the handling of boats difficult. Although this stretch abounded in sharp turns, the canal was so high above the surrounding countryside that approaching craft could be clearly seen, which meant that there was no need for someone to be on the towpath with the horse all the time.

When horse-boats met, the one which did not have right of way would stop so that the other horse could walk over the tow-line. in theory the boat with right of way would take the inside and sail over the dropped line of the other. This was the official BCN rule, but actual practice was for the outside boat to 'clear' his line over the top of the other, hoping that it would not get caught round the mast or catch the chimney and can. This routine accounted for the expression: "'Eave it up!", and in the days of heavy horse-drawn traffic you might be 'eaving it up all day long. Actually the situation was not quite as bad as that because the newer parts of the B.C.N. had towpaths on each side. In any case, most boats followed the pattern of making their way out to the collieries in the morning and returning later in the day, therefore not meeting head on. It was on sections of the canal close to the collieries that the most frequent meetings occurred, as the first boats to come out obviously had to cross the remainder of the incoming boats. It was for this reason that the Cannock Extension Canal, known locally as the 'Edgeford (Hednesford) Arm, was often referred to as the "Eavitup".

The approach to Rushall was marked by a number of disused cement, brick and lime works. It was from here that the cement for building the huge Nechells Power Station in Birmingham had been transported by boat. The villages of Rushall and Daw End are more or less the same place, and thereafter the canal wound through green fields to reach its terminus in a basin near Longwood. Shortly before the end of the Daw End Branch the Rushall Canal began, at the top of two locks known as the Top of Mosses. There were stables here, and in fact it was not far from the centre of Walsall, though it always gave the appearance from the canal of being in deep countryside.

Below Mosses there was a mile pound before the seven Rushall Locks, which were known as the Ganzy. Halfway down the flight is a basin and "The Bell" pub. This was the route taken by boats from the Cannock collieries to the busy industrial area of Aston, commemorated in the jingle:

"Mosses Two, Ganzy Seven,
The New Thirteen and the Lousy 'Leven."

The Lousy 'Leven referred to the eleven locks of the Aston flight – awkward to work and extremely congested – and not the combined Saltley and Camp Hill locks.

The Rushall Canal was one of the more recently built parts of the B.C.N. and ran perfectly straight from Longwood to its right angled junction with the Tame Valley Canal (known as the New Cut) at Newtown Junction. It was a difficult turn, the space available barely exceeding the length of the boat. To negotiate it you threw the bight of the line over the the fore stud, then put it behind a pulley fixed on the bank for that purpose so that the horse could pull the fore end round. The steerer had to position the boat carefully to start with and then row the tiller vigorously. In spite of all this effort boats often hit the opposite wall, in fact this was so common that we didn't even bother to swear!

The New Cut was a magnificent waterway. Starting at Salford Junction (Gravelly Hill) it climbed to Perry Barr by thirteen deep locks, and thence ran in an almost straight line to its junction with the Walsall Canal at Ocker Hill. Strongly walled throughout, and with a towpath on both sides, it was a canal of cuttings and embankments, which had once been rural throughout. Unfortunately it was now lined for much of its length by housing estates, the inhabitants of which had found it to be a convenient dumping ground for unwanted rubbish, whilst their children were apt to while away the time by hurling missiles at passing boatmen.

Magnificent as the New Cut was, it had the drawback of being very shallow. It was understandable that the canal engineers would not want to keep much depth on the embanked sections, as the greater the depth the more pressure and risk of a 'blow-out' or breach. In the Friars Park cutting, heavy rain would wash sand into the cut and the movement of boats would tend to spread the silting effect of this. There were a number of rubbish tips alongside the canal and it was to be expected that some of this would find its way into the water to join the domestic refuse from nearby houses. Of course this lack of depth was not so noticeable with a slow moving horse boat, but it was painful with a motor, especially as the long straight stretches, walled to prevent bank erosion, positively invited one to open the throttle.

Once round Newtown Junction we were on a high embankment with an extensive tip to our right, on which we could see several 'tatters' at work. These were men who combed tips in search of 'tat', the most prized items being bits of brass and copper. Each tatter had his own pitch which he guarded jealously, and we soon came to recognise individual 'tatters' cycling to work with clockwork regularity, or returning home with the day's gleanings in a bag on the carrier. These would be sold to a local scrap merchant like the one close to the cut at Salford Bridge, which incidentally still survives today. Boatmen too, never neglected to pick up a bit of tat, and it made a useful addition to our earnings.

Coming off the embankment on to an aqueduct, we crossed the Grand Junction line of the London Midland Region, getting a bird's eye view of the entrance to the enormous Bescot marshalling yards. Then came the Walsall Road at Stone Cross, where thirsty boatmen could nip down the bank for a quick pint before plunging into the deep cutting at Friars Park. High bridges spanned this cutting from which local children would pelt passing boats with every kind of missile, secure in the knowledge that the boatmen could not possibly reach them. Whilst this sort of behaviour was unknown in the older communities along the B.C.N., passing through the new housing estates was something to be dreaded, and also the constant accumulation of rubbish soon reduced payloads and eventually made parts of the B.C.N. almost impassable. It always seemed to me most unfair that British Waterways should have been required to bear the cost of dredging and raking these sections of canal. It should have fallen fairly and squarely on the local authorities whose tenants were responsible.

It was always a relief to clear Friars Park and to emerge on to the Hateley Heath embankment which, although there was a large housing estate on the left hand side, was reasonably trouble-free, though the towpath tended to be haunted by old ladies who would threaten to report us for: "letting that poor horse pull that great big boat." On the other side of the canal there were extensive views across the infant Tame towards Wednesbury. In those days the Tame had the reputation of being England's most polluted river. Beyond Holloway Bank bridge the first canalside industry on the Tame Valley began to appear, increasing as we slid through Goldshill Stop where the toll collector's house was right up against what was then a very busy and noisy railway line.

Joey boats were unloading at the works on the right hand side, which was pointed out to me as the famous 'Shadow Factory' from which many a boat-load of shell casings had been despatched during the war. They would arrive at their destination in a highly polished state due to the rotation imparted by the vibration of Bolinder engines. Crossing an area of typical Black Country wasteland, where footpaths wound through the pools and hillocks of old mine-workings, massive cooling towers denoted our approach to the junction with the Walsall Canal at Ocker Hill. With our horse crossing the canal by a turnover bridge, we turned left, and leaving the junction with the Tipton Green & Toll End Communication Canal on our right, and passing the junctions of two branch canals and the railway transhipment basin at Great Bridge, we slid into the uninviting chamber of the bottom lock of the Ryders Green flight, known as the West Bromwich Eight.

By 1954, only single boats and pairs used this route, for despite having more locks it was quicker than going via Wolverhampton. But back in the 1930s, before the introduction of motor tugs diverted local coal traffic to the longer route via Wolverhampton (giving a lock-free run to Smethwick and access to the Birmingham Level with only three locks) this had been the most notorious bottleneck on the B.C.N. All the coal traffic from the Cannock coalfield, approaching both via The Ganzy and via the Walsall Canal, had to be funnelled through here if it was bound for Oldbury, Smethwick, 'Upper' Birmingham, West Bromwich, and the Worcester and Stratford canals. Maximum capacity was seven boats per hour in each direction, there were long queues, and tempers were apt to be frayed, quite understandably as the local boatmen, not living aboard their craft, wished to get finished and go home as soon as possible. Time spent waiting turn at locks was not paid for, and while some Joey boats had a cosy little cabin, others were completely open with only a fire bucket to keep the crew warm. At the top and bottom of these locks were open-fronted shelters with curved corrugated-iron roofs where you could tie your horse and get out of the rain, but the canal company's rules for 'taking turn' required the boatmen to be on their boat, the horse pegged to, and the tiller inserted. Lengthy notices outlining these and other rules were displayed at all flights on the B.C.N. There was also an unwritten custom whereby each boatman would say to the one in front: "I take turn to you." Boatmen who could recall those days would tell me that if you hadn't started work by five o'clock in the morning you might as well stay at home all day.

West Bromwich Eight were not the cleanest of locks, nor the most convenient to work, being rather short and having single bottom gates. This meant that when the gate was being closed it would rub against the boat's 'elum', the scrubbed ropework on which would have to be protected by covering it with a sack. However there were plenty of B.C.N. locks which were worse, and at least they had the merit of being quick to work. The flight was lined with industry, the metal working variety giving place to chemical plants as you neared the top.

An Ernie Thomas horse-boat, bound for the Wellington Tube Works half way up the locks, was in front of us, and we met another coming down loaded with rubbish for Moxley Tip, working frantically to keep ahead of an empty Element's. As we neared the top the air smelled strongly of formaldehyde, this being one of the principal products of the area, from whence it was transported by boat to Langley Green.

When you emerged from the top of Ryder's Green locks in those days, it was on to a waterway completely enclosed by factories stretching as far as the eye could reach. It was about a mile to the junction with the Main Line at Pudding Green. Arms and basins abounded, in some of which could be seen the shapes of craft loading and discharging. At the Albion Station Arm we encountered a sight for sore eyes, an ex Shropshire Union boat, the *Hogarth*, beautifully turned out in a glossy black and white livery and piled high with crates. Passing Lee's rolling mill, whose front was open to the canal so that you could see the activity within, and a basin where R.B. Tudor's boats were unloading house coal, we turned on to the familiar waters of the Main Line. The course of the Wednesbury Old Canal on which we had been travelling, continued across to form Izon Turn, a weedy waterway where mysterious things which we could not quite make out seemed to go on.

A little further on we came to Bromford Stop with its island toll house where *Thomas* was brought to a stand to be gauged. The toll clerk came out with his gauging stick and placed it on each of four metal plates, two on each side of the boat, reading off the 'dry inches', or freeboard, in each position. The figures were averaged and the load calculated by reference to the boat's individual gauging table of which each toll house kept a copy. Ray was handed a copy of the toll ticket and away we went, taking the right hand towpath for the rest of the journey into Birmingham.

Next day *Thomas* and her crew had a long day's work in front of them. Bob was pegged to at 6 a.m. and hauled us to Kings Norton Tunnel where the tunnel tug was waiting to tow us to Tardebigge. The descent of the 'Thirty-Twelve' (the 42 locks to the bottom of Astwood) was accomplished in short order. Lock-keepers were bribed with cash or coal to set the road in advance of us so that each lock was ready. As the fore-end of the boat entered each lock, the steerer cried: "Draw!", and the opened paddle sucked the boat in at a great rate. Poised in the hatches at the stern, the steerer removed the great wooden tiller and, seizing his strap, dropped the bight of it over the iron-shod strapping post which extended upwards from the top gate. Swiftly taking a turn round the boat's stern stud, he skillfully brought it to a stand just short of the bottom gates. By the time we reached the foot of Astwood, the stern stud was polished to such a brilliance that you could see your face in it. The 'driver', having completed drawing the paddles, attached the block rope to its peg set in the offside copings. This rope led back through a pulley on the mast, and was connected to the tow-line so that the horse had the benefit of a 2:1 purchase when starting the boat out of the lock. A wooden peg limited its run, and caused it to drop slack and fall off the lockside peg of its own accord. This was boating at its most satisfying: the rattle of paddles, the slam of gates, the urgent cries of "Whoa!", "Gee-up!", and "Draw!", and the still water flowering into turbulence as 25,000 gallons was released from each lock.

Below Astwood there was a complete change of pace. We entered a five mile pound, the sides fringed with rushes so tall and thick, that all that could be seen was the tow-line disappearing into them. Out of sight was Bob, quietly 'backering' along by himself as we relaxed with sandwiches and cups of tea. Sometimes fishermen would be ensconced in the 'segs', their peaceful hobby disturbed by the unexpected equine shape, dragging its wet and filthy tow-line which would sometimes drop slack and entwine itself in their tackle, only to tauten again scattering bait and baskets far and wide. At Dunhampstead Tunnel, which had no towpath, one of us disembarked to urge Bob on to greater speed, so as to give us a good start before we needed to pull the boat through using an iron handrail. After leaving Dunhampstead's spider infested depths, Bob could be relied upon to keep up a steady pace, as he knew he was approaching his stable at 'Parkers' (Offerton) Locks.

It took only a few hours to complete the voyage to Worcester on the following day. Around 10 a.m. Bob was un-pegged for the last time and *Thomas* would glide to its berth at the mill. Now the shovels would be brought out to unload the coal into its very restricted storage space, a tedious task for which an extra hand was always welcome. After we had unloaded at Townsend's, I bade farewell to *Thomas* and caught the train back to Tamworth. My week with Ray had introduced me to parts of the canal system previously unknown and of quite unsuspected fascination, and I had been privileged to travel them on what was then almost the last long distance horse-boat in England.

CHAPTER THREE

LONGFORD
LIGHT

·

My return to Tamworth found *New Hope* ready to be re-launched, her hull glistening with fresh tar and cabin-side lettering proudly proclaiming:

THOS. FOXON, CANAL CARRIER, BRAUNSTON.

I had already painted the exterior of the cabin and engine hole in a shade known as Ayr Red, which was separated from an oak grained surround by green mouldings. The lettering was white, shaded with ochre. The boat's name and her Grand Union gauging number appeared on the side of the engine hole.

The boat was jacked up and the packing removed, after which she was lowered on to the greased, iron shod timbers of the slipway and allowed to slide into the water with a satisfying splash. Bow-hauling the short distance to Ted Jones' dock, I returned to S.E. Barlow's office to arrange for a load as soon as the engine was ready. Mr Barlow, known as 'Little Sam', was the 'bottom end' agent for the Warwickshire Boat Control which organised the loading of boats at all the Warwickshire collieries and quarries, and also at Measham on the Ashby Canal. Headquarters of the Boat Control was at Sutton's Stop (Hawkesbury Junction), the officer in charge being Mr Shaw, assisted by Miss Edwards. The whole system was increadibly cumbersome, the number of boats loaded each day in the entire Warwickshire coalfield being less than one loading place alone in the Cannock area could handle.

'S.E.' was a portly, middle-aged man with a quirky sense of humour. On one occasion the crew of one of his Joey boats asked me to call in and give him a message that their horse wouldn't eat. "That's all right," he remarked: "It'll cost me less to keep." Boatwomen collecting rope from the stores, were accustomed to having a strap, held six inches from the end, waved at them with the straight-faced enquiry: "How much would you like?" S.E. was well-liked on the cut and I have the happiest memories of working for him. He could afford to be easy going, because his secretary, the redoubtable Miss Hall, ran the business with an iron hand and an acid tongue, and it was a brave boatman who dared to cross swords with her.

"What are you going to do?" asked Sam, and I told him that I expected to load for Banbury Co-op when the boat was ready. I was taken aback when he told me that that month's allocation had already been filled. "But you can go on the 'Coventry Light' job," he offered. Coventry Light was Longford Power Station, situated just beyond the junction of the Coventry and Oxford canals at Hawkesbury. Loading at Pooley Hall Colliery, this was a short distance run, "A Joey boat job," I thought contemptuously to myself, not at all the romantic long distance voyaging I had been looking forward to. However, I agreed to go on it for a while, at a rate of 3/9d per ton, anticipating that I would be able to do three trips per week. Ted Jones didn't take long to weld the crack in the cylinder block. On May 22nd, 1954 we carried out successful trials and the following day, at 7.20 p.m., I set off under my own power for Pooley Hall.

Getting *New Hope* ready for trade had taken longer than I anticipated, and I was thankful to be starting work at last. Priming the engine I swung the starting handle, knocked over the decompression lever, known to us as the 'lifter', and the National coughed and spluttered into life. I let go the fore-end and stern strings, turned the gear wheel to engage forward gear, and cautiously opened the throttle. The hull trembled and I felt the 'elum' grip the water as the boat moved forward. Waving goodbye to the Jones's, I lit a cigarette and poured out a cup of tea. At last, I felt, my career as a Number One had really begun.

It was only a forty-five minute run from Glascote to Pooley and I didn't hurry, wishing to savour the sensation of being back at the tiller. A narrowboat is steered from the footboard, which projects into the cabin and can be enclosed by shutting the cabin doors behind you. You are then standing in a small space, about two feet square, which extends upwards to somewhere between hips and waist. Just below the steerer's feet on the left hand side is the top of the range, which not only keeps him warm, but allows the making of tea and some cooking to be done while in motion.

Just before Pooley was a low bridge, for which the chimney had to be taken off its collar and laid flat on the cabin top, and the mast to be unfastened and propped up against the mast beam at an angle. The loading chutes lay behind an island in the cut forming a lay-by into which I turned and tied up. No other cabin boats were moored there, only a handful of

Joey boats awaiting loading or collection in the morning.

Stopping the engine, I went below and had a wash before preparing supper. This over, and the washing up done, I filled in my log book and made the bed. Before turning in I stood on the coal box and, arms resting on the cabin top, enjoyed a last cup of tea and a cigarette while contemplating the scene around me. It was dark and the boats and loading gear were only dim shapes in the gloom. There was no sound from the pit head to remind me of the men and ponies labouring in the bowels of the earth, but every few seconds a pipe projecting over the canal bank emitted a cloud of steam and a weary sigh. Pooley Hall that night was an atmospheric place and, more so than at any time since returning to England, I felt very close to the heart of the canal.

"New Hope ahoy!*"*

I had nearly finished breakfast next morning when the boat loaders arrived. Looking out I saw two men, one thin, the other short and plump. Their names, I discovered, were George and Ernie. I put the boat under the chute while the first wagon of coal was placed in position, its drawgear attached to a hoist which up-ended it so that the coal poured out through its end door into the hopper. The hopper outlet was controlled by a shutter worked by a big iron lever. George pushed down on the lever, the shutter opened, and a stream of pea slack descended into the hold. All I had to do was move her backwards and forwards by pushing on the gunwale with my feet so as to get the required trim.

It had been years since *New Hope* had a cargo in her, and I expected that she would leak before the timbers eventually took up, so I put in what I estimated was a load of only 18 tons. We could see water running in, so Ernie came to the rescue with that time honoured expedient, ashes, of which they had plenty in their hovel. These were sprinkled on the water around the boat, the theory being that they would be drawn into the leaks and help to plug them. I wasn't used to dealing with leaky boats, all my previous craft having been, as they say, 'fit for bagged stuff', so I didn't know that in such circumstances it was wise to leave a 'lade-hole'. This is a space left in the cargo, behind the mast and down to the floorboards, so that if necessary the boatman can get in there armed with a bucket and get the water out. When the weight had been calculated, the ticket showed 21 tons 6 cwt. *New Hope* was obviously a bigger boat than I had thought as she had about a plank and a half of dry side.

Putting up the deckboard – decorated with its scrubbed white belting – and the fore-plank, I laid the rest of the planks on top of the coal, disdaining to fasten them to the top of the stands and support them with uprights for such a short trip. At 8 a.m. I started the engine, putting the bilge pump on, let go and headed south with my first load.

To my mind the National engine had little to commend it, but an exception must be made for the bilge pump which was both reliable and effective. The pump kept the cabin and engine room bilges clear, but could not work on the water in the hold which, because the boat was loaded slightly by the head, all ran forward whilst the pump intake was at the back end of the hold. Although I could tell that the boat was leaking quite a lot, I couldn't actually see the bottom of the hold because of the coal, and I never thought to open the deck lid and look in. However, the trip proceeded without incident, albeit rather slowly as my recollections of this bit of the canal were hazy and I had to feel my way, until, at 5.45 in the afternoon, *New Hope* came to a stand in Vernons Lane bridge at Nuneaton. Forward, she had dropped down 'into the paint', and I when I opened the deck lid I was horrified to see that the water had reached about a foot below the gunwhale. For a moment I was panic stricken, until I realised that, as she was on the bottom, she was in no danger of sinking, and that, moreover, she was in an ideal position to be pumped out by the fire brigade. There was a phone box nearby and it was not long before they arrived, lowered a hose into the deck and pumped the water out in short order, a service which cost me 24/-. At 8.30 I started up again and tied up at Bedworth two hours later. After fifteen hours under cargo, *New Hope* appeared to be sealing up quite well.

The boat didn't make a lot of water overnight, and by half past eight the next morning I was tied up at The Light. There were a number of boats waiting to unload. One of the boatmen there was Bill Dale. He operated a pair of S.E. Barlow's and was also responsible for a number of Joey boats which he worked between Newdigate Colliery and the power station. Because he had to deal with these boats, Bill had a motor pump, and we gave *New Hope* a thorough pumping out. Slack absorbs water like a sponge, mine had been saturated and we were now getting the water that was draining out of it. It was the following morning that I went into the length to be unloaded (so much for my expectations of doing three trips a week) and there was a great deal of complaint about the slack being so wet, the unloading operation taking much longer than usual.

There was nowhere to wind at The Light, and enquiries revealed that it was necessary to go to the junction with the disused Wyken Old Arm, where you put your stern under the side bridge and shafted the fore-end round. The water under the bridge was full of bricks from the half-demolished parapet and you had to be careful not to catch the propellor. In any wind this was a very difficult place to turn, about the worse I ever had to use. Successfully winded, I had got back as far as Tushes Bridge when there was an ominous clatter from the engine. I stopped, tied up and sent for Mr Jones. It was the next day but one when the repair was completed, a big end having run out. I ran the engine during the morning of the following day, but no sooner had I untied than there was a bang and the engine stopped. Bill Dale happened to be there and he quickly whipped off the cylinder head. On the top of a National's piston is an object rather like the top of a Brasso bottle. This had worked loose, hit the cylinder head and smashed the crown of the piston. Yet another entry in my log, "Sent for fitter."

This had happened on the 29th May and it was the 1st June before the engine was repaired. I oiled up 10 gallons of fuel, all I could afford, let go at 4.30 p.m. and tied up at Baddesley five hours later, arriving at Pooley at 7.10 the next morning. My first trip had taken nine days and had earned me £3.19s.10d gross.

Loading was immediate and by 8.30 I was on my way back to Longford with 21 tons 8 cwt of coal. I had decided to load slightly by the stern so as to enable the bilge pump to work on the hold while going along. This proved to be unnecessary – after her thorough soaking *New Hope* had taken up nicely and, although never exactly a bone dry boat when loaded, gave no more trouble in this direction. Down by the stern she was murder to steer, as are all narrowboats in this condition, but I was getting along nicely until, negotiating a sharp bend near White Hall Farm, I got too close to the outside bank. There was a nasty bang under the counter and the propellor ceased to revolve. Picking up the cabin floor board I found what I had feared, a broken coupling between the intermediate and the propellor shafts. These couplings were made of cast iron and broke very easily, which was why in many cases, shear pins had been fitted to prevent this, the soft metal pin through coupling and shaft being easily replaced, but this had not been done to *New Hope*. There was nothing for me to do but beg a tow to Hartshill behind Ron Wilson and send for the ever obliging Mr Jones who obtained a new coupling from British Waterways at Hatton and drilled it and the shaft to take a shear pin.

This incident illustrates the need for boatmen to 'know the road' intimately. I had only been over this bit of canal three times, and two of these occasions had been four years previously. Had I known of an underwater obstruction, I could have pulled out of gear had I thought I was anywhere close to it.

I was now beginning to know some of the boatmen who worked to The

Autumn afternoon, Brownhills.

Late shift at the railway basin.

Light. Apart from Bill Dale, S.E. Barlow had two pairs regularly trading there from Pooley, captained by Dick Littlemore and Bill Humphries. Both had been displaced from the longer distance Oxford trade and I was told that no boats at all now went there. The Samuel Barlow Coal Co. had one pair dedicated to the traffic, their coal being loaded at Measham on the Ashby Canal, supplemented by other boats as required. The Measham to Longford run, because of its absence of locks, was more or less reserved for the very aged or for pregnant women, being known as the 'babby length'. It was not unknown for a boatwoman who felt in need of a rest to stick a pillow under her dress and go marching into the office demanding to be put on the babby length.

Also trading to The Light was Joe Skinner, last of the horse-drawn owner-boatmen on the Coventry and Oxford canals. This was only a filling-in job for Joe, as he carried to Banbury Dairy, which burnt at least two loads of coal each month, and also made a monthly trip with house coal to Banbury Wharf.

I was too late to load before the Whitsun holiday which I spent at Polesworth. Loading on the 9th June, I was caught in the Whitsun maintenance stoppage at Atherstone Locks, which was scheduled to finish at eight o'clock that evening. All the delays had been unprofitable financially, and my performance so far had been rather shaming for someone who aspired to make a name for himself as a fast worker, so I decided that as soon as the stoppage was finished I would start up and work straight through to Longford. The stoppage lifted at 6.30 p.m. and away I went up the locks. It was a beautiful summer's evening and when I reached Mancetter I found Mike and Polly Rogers tied up there with *Mabel*, now converted into a hotel boat. I had known the Rogers when they carried coal in *Mabel*, and had often visited them when I had been stationed at RAF Hendon. This being the first time I had come across them since my return to The Cut, I stopped for a chat. We reminisced about the old days: "Coal is so much less trouble than passengers," said Polly. Eventually I had to get going again: "Boatman's itch," laughed Mike.

New Hope didn't boast a headlight, but there was a good moon and I was able to toddle along round the Atherstone Pound without difficulty, thoroughly enjoying myself in the process. By one in the morning I had lost the moon so decided to tie up at the Moira Cut End, but seeing a pair of Barlow's moored on the Ashby side of the lock, I made sure of getting away early in the morning. There were no other boats at The Light, so I went straight into the length, emptied, winded, and was back at Sutton's by 10.30. When Miss Edwards, the assistant boat controller, rang her colleague at Glascote, the dragon-like Miss Hall, she was greeted with astonishment. "Empty? He can't be. He hasn't got there yet!" This pleased me no end, and I was even more gratified when , meeting Bill Humphries in the pound below Baddesley, his son, Mike, commented: "You must have bloody wings!"

The next trip was uneventful and noteworthy only for the fact that I did it in the proper time of 8 ½ hours with a load of 22 tons 17 cwt. But although I arrived on a Thursday, I didn't get unloaded until the following Monday. It had now become quite clear that it was impossible to do more than two trips per week because of the delays in unloading. Two trips would gross about £8.10/- a week, giving an estimated net income of £4 or £5. If not very profitable, at least there was little wear and tear, and it would be prudent to stay on this run for a while as it was convenient in case of any engine trouble. Eventually I expected to have some loads for Banbury Co-op, but at 12/6d per ton, including unloading with a shovel and barrow, this was not very much more attractive financially. I was worried about my outstanding bills for docking (about £26) and engine repairs (about £10) though, had I given the matter some thought, I would have realised that they could have been paid off by a small amount each week as was customary procedure for Number Ones. As it was, I wanted a few quick, profitable loads to restore my financial equilibrium and also, running up and down between Pooley Hall and Longford Power Station still seemed, to my mind, a Joey boat job, and I hankered for what I then considered to be the more satisfying long distance work.

It was with some excitement then, that when I picked up my mail at Sutton's, I found a letter from the North West Division of British Waterways quoting a list of sub-contract rates and suggesting that on my way down there I should contact the Mersey, Weaver and Ship Canal Carrying Company for a load north from the Potteries. Calculating that a load from Burslem to Manchester, followed by another from Manchester to Birmingham, would bring me a quick £25, and having itchy feet anyway, I set sail for the Mersey.

CHAPTER FOUR

THE NORTH
STAFFORD

•

It was well into the afternoon when *New Hope* set out from Glascote on her journey towards that part of the canal system so bound up with my earliest days on The Cut. At Fazeley Junction, where Element's and Barlow's open boats from Baddesley and Pooley turned left towards Birmingham, I forged straight ahead, entering a world of almost deserted waters. Since the cessation in 1953 of the regular chemical traffic carried from Manchester to Courtauld's artificial fibre works at Coventry by Cowburn & Cowpar, and the end of the Bournville to Nottingham boats, only very occasional cargoes of grain from Manchester to Southall, and timber to Old Ford on the Hertford Union Canal, had disturbed the placid waters between Fazeley and Fradley.

The eleven miles between Fazeley and Fradley was pleasant enough, the canal winding gently northwards, as it followed the valley of the Tame towards its confluence with the Trent. Apart from the village of Hopwas, from which a market boat once ran to Birmingham, there was only an occasional cottage or pub beside the canal. This unfrequented air was in decided contrast to the busy part of the Coventry Canal which ran through the more populated Warwickshire coalfield. There was not much depth of water, but this was not as noticeable with an empty boat as with a loaded one, and I boated peacefully along. Hay time had yet to come and young cows ran down through flowery pastures to investigate the noisy intruder. Beneath the green leaved towpath hedge, entwined with convolvulous, honeysuckle and dog roses, the grass had been left to grow high. Before long the meadows gave way to the extensive woods of Hopwas Hays, their inviting cool green depths and bracken fringed paths studded with notices warning of the dangers of the Army firing range.

Five and a half miles from Fazeley came the invisible boundary between the Divisions, and with it deep water. While I had been away, the North Western Division had thoroughly dredged the canal between Whittington

Brook and Fradley, and it was now in first class condition. I had not expected to meet any boats, so it was a pleasant surprise to encounter an ex Josher 'pup' charging along at a great rate with a load of grain for Kelloggs factory at Southall. She was smartly clothed up and bedecked with every traditional decoration of scrubbed rope, woodwork and polished brass that her young captain could devise. We exchanged greetings as he slid by, Bolinder thumping rhythmically, our last words almost drowned in the racket of a 'pup' at 450 revs after he had bent down to shove in his oil rod. Not for the first time I thought what a marvellous life boating was: fresh air and exercise, no one to bother you, a constantly changing scene unfolding before your eyes, and at night a mooring by some cosy pub. But, of course, boating wasn't always such a peaceful and uneventful occupation, so an afternoon like this was to be savoured.

Whittington, at that time a village of almost negligible proportions, slid by, to be followed by a wooden bridge, the turnover bridge for Huddlesford Junction. Here a narrow strip of water between thick beds of reeds led off towards Lichfield whose cathedral spires towered above the meadows. This was the Wyrley & Essington Canal and rumour had it that the Ogley Locks section of it was either closed or about to be closed. Not far from the junction, this flight of thirty locks started their climb to the 473 feet Wolverhampton level only seven miles away, and it was hard to imagine that such a short distance from sleepy Huddlesford, a continuous stream of coal laden tug 'trains' and horse-boats was on the move from the collieries high on Cannock Chase. There had been little traffic over the five mile section between Pipe Hill waterworks and Huddlesford for years, whilst the Cannock – Pipe Hill traffic had ceased in 1952. Who was to know, that within a year or two, coal traffic would be flowing from Cannock to London, and that this route would have been the quickest and least heavily locked. From Anglesey Basin to Braunston there were 47 locks in 60 miles via Huddlesford and no less than 84 locks in 59 miles via Salford Junction and Warwick. Many a boatman trudging the mucky towpath through Birmingham with a gritty, grease laden line over his shoulder as he, or more likely she, bow-hauled a heavily laden butty was to bemoan the closure of Ogley Locks.

There were four more rural miles beyond Huddlesford until, skirting the wartime aerodrome to which RAF stores were boated during the war, and with her wash lapping the edge of Fradley Wood, *New Hope* came to Fradley. I tied up to the well-worn rings outside "The Swan" public house which stands guard over this meeting place of waterways from Thames, Mersey and Trent. It was a sleepy place, accessible only by a strip of widened, unsurfaced towpath leading from a tangle of country lanes. There were a couple of houses and the canal maintenance yard, but the nearest shop was two miles distant. It needs a considerable stretch of imagination to remember just how isolated, in the 1950s, some canal locations could be. It was the contrast of these remote spots with busier waters elsewhere that was part of the charm of The Cut.

In scenic terms the location of Fradley Junction was an enviable one, but in the bar that evening the landlord bemoaned the loss of trade. It had been a fortnight since a pair of boats had tied up outside, pausing for the night before delivering their cargo of milk powder to Leicester. He remembered when John Knill's fleet had traded salt along the canal and we recalled a evening in the winter of 1951. Whilst on leave from the RAF, I had taken the train to Rugeley to join *Columba* and *Kenelm* southbound with salt for Reading. We had dropped down the locks at Fradley to find a small group of boats stopped for the night, smoke drifting skywards from their cabin fires in the frosty air which was redolent with the smell of cooking. There had been a Coventry bound Cowburn & Cowpar with its hazardous cargo of carbon disulphide; a pair of London boats en route from Bournville to Nottingham; and my erstwhile youthful mentor, Arthur 'Brunjie' Harris, a Severn & Canal man who had ended up in the North West, and who had been on his way to Nottingham with a load of cardboard destined to make cartons for Player's cigarettes. Arthur was buttied by a pair of Northern boats captained by the redoubtable Ike Wilson of Kidderminster, ably assisted by his wife Emmie and daughter Mim.

Supper over, we had drifted into the pub. To have seven boats tied up at Fradley was an unusual occasion and one to celebrate. After a few pints the London captain brought out 'the music', as boatmen call the accordion. Soon the room was full of song, interspersed by demonstrations of clog dancing on the table top. As pint had followed pint, the almost obsolete ceremony of proposing a toast to 'The Trade' took place, to which we had all heartily assented. Had we foreseen the years to come we might well have followed it with: "Damnation to the Road Hauliers." But we boatmen were tolerant folk, quite prepared to live and let live.

As the bar grew hotter and more smokey, some of the young ladies pleaded the need for fresh air, and were escorted outside by a sheepish boat youth or farm hand. They returned some time later blushful and happy but not as bashful as their escorts, who had to submit to the ritual of having their fingernails examined by the older men for shreds of nylon. All too soon came closing time, although it was rarely enforced with exactitude in such country places. Nobody had seemed in a hurry to go to bed and we stayed outside for some time before dispersing. The evening's activities were not over however, Arthur wanted a rabbit for the stewpot, and nothing would serve but that I should accompany him while he put down some snares. I didn't get up until his engine started in the morning, but I poked my head out in time to see two rabbits dangling down from the cabin side.

This had only been a few years ago but now only the unladen *New Hope* occupied the moorings outside the pub. The landlord told me that without the custom of Black Country fishermen at weekends he would find it hardly worth opening. Little could he have forseen that the era of mass car ownership and increased trade for country pubs was about to dawn, followed a few years later by a cut crammed with pleasure boats.

Northbound boats faced three locks on leaving Fradley, of the deep Trent & Mersey design but perfectly convenient for single-handed uphill working. The Trent & Mersey was known to Midlands boatmen as the 'North Stafford' after the railway company which once owned it. In those days there were still N.S.R. notices at various points along the canal. Ownership had been advantageous to the railway, enabling it to greatly expand its traffic catchment area. There were several basins where traffic could be transhipped between canal and rail, including one at Willington at the eastern extremity of the N.S.R.'s rails. This allowed it to compete for traffic from Derby and Nottingham as well as that coming up the River Trent.

Immediately on leaving Fradley I passed through Shades House and Wood End locks, these being followed by a fairly long, tree shaded pound to Bromley Common, where begins a level pound, of about nine miles, to Colwich. Bracken and foxgloves fringed the water, but over towards the Trent lay wide acres dotted by solid and prosperous looking farm houses. The North Stafford could well have been called the 'Rhododendron Cut', for Ravenshaw Wood was thick with these shrubs and they also appear near Great Haywood, around Stone and further north beyond Middlewich in the Big Lock pound.

Beyond Ravenshaw Wood lies more open country and the heights of Cannock Chase dominate the western horizon, but it is not long before the industrial settlements of Handsacre and Armitage are approached. Some may describe such places as depressing, but without industry there would have been no canal. The more enquiring may strike a rich seam of human interest, for it was from villages like this that D.H. Lawrence obtained much of his material. Handsacre once had its own boating community which included the legendary Steve Dulson, the last man to work a horse boat on the Shropshire Union. One of his daughters had the distinction of having fourteen children, some of whom I knew well. There was a canalside pub at Handsacre where I had several memorable evenings. Armitage had a roadstone wharf and a large canalside works making sanitary pottery, once a customer of the canal but by this time prone to silt it up with the discharge of its clayey effluent. Here was to be encountered the 130 yard Plum Pudding Tunnel, which L.T.C. Rolt, when he travelled this way in 1939, described as more nearly representing a natural cavern, because of the rough and ready way it had been hacked through a sandstone outcrop with the crude implements of the early navigators.

Armitage is not far distant from Rugeley, but first comes the disused Brereton Colliery basin, the path of whose tramroad ran straight and steep to its mine high up on The Chase. I wrote somewhat of Rugeley in my first book, "Anderton for Orders", and it will suffice to say that the intervening five years had not improved its aspect from the water. However I greeted the slaughterhouse and tannery as old friends and mentally saluted the bridge where we always got stuck with the salt boats. But there was something new to see in the shape of Lea Hall Colliery and the adjoining power station. Situated right beside a waterway which led to power stations at Meaford (15 miles) and Willington (22 miles), the failure to provide loading facilities and to use the canal to carry its coal was a depressing commentary on the sterility of the transport policy of the day. Of what avail had it been for the Government of 1945 to bring into public ownership coal, power and transport? For an answer one had only to look at the growing numbers and ever increasing size of the privately owned lorries at pit head and power station.

As Purgatory is said to be the necessary prelude to Paradise, so the passage of Rugeley must be deemed to enhance the enjoyment of the next stretch of canal. I had crossed the Trent by the abrupt right-angled turn known as Brindley's Bank, where a youthful boatman had once sacrificed a number of *Columba*'s sheer pins negotiating it in the dark, and now the land rose gently on my right towards Chartley Great Park, then still a thinly populated and little known part of the country. Across the Trent, winding through its quiet pastures, lay the steep slopes of Cannock Chase, which at Bishton closely approaches the canal. So peaceful was the scene, and so devoid of boats the canal, that the mind baulked at the thought that, only five miles to the south, lay Hednesford Basin, terminus of the Cannock Extension Canal, 473 feet above sea level and loading upwards of fifty boats each day. But here, approaching the solitary lock at Colwich,

New Hope was in deep countryside, completely remote from industry and commerce. Above Colwich a pound of about a mile led to Haywood Lock beyond which lay Haywood Junction, even more deserted than that at Fradley, where the canal from the Severn joined the 'North Stafford'. Haywood is also a junction of rivers, for the Trent and Sow unite here just above an attractive packhorse bridge.

There are only four locks in the nine miles that separates Haywood from Stone, a town that was closely associated with the canal from its inception, being the headquarters of both the canal company and of Hugh Henshall, a firm which was for all practical purposes the canal company in its guise as a carrier, canal companies not being allowed to act as carriers in the early days of the canals. There were drydocks at Stone being used by British Waterways to maintain some of the boats of their North Western fleet. An old friend, the single motor *Gambia*, Saltley built as a butty in 1907 for Fellows, Morton & Clayton, was there sitting high and dry on the blocks. Some dockyards managed to make an attractive job of the British Waterways blue and yellow livery, but Stone was not one of them. *Gambia*'s cabinside looked terrible, and I couldn't help thinking how attractive she had looked when I had first seen her tied up at Sherborne Street wharf in her Fellows Morton colours. Stone was also the headquarters of an early holiday cruising firm. There were already one or two hire cruisers available on The Cut but the number never became substantial during my own career as a boatman.

I had seen no sign of trade since the boat I had met at Huddlesford, so it was with some excitement that I noted a fresh pile of china clay on the wharf of the pottery works above the top lock and hoped that it had been delivered there by boat. That this was the case was evidenced by the fact that the four locks at Meaford had been left full with the top gates open. Normally on little used canals, the lock-keepers would close the top gates, after which leakage through the bottom gates would start to drain the chamber. A small heap of fresh ashes was another indication that a boat had gone up not far in front of me.

There can be few more pleasant settings than that of Meaford Locks climbing gently up their grassy slope set about with trees. Above the top lock lay an enormous power station, separated from the canal by a network of sidings and yet, being only a couple of miles from the loading wharf of Sideway Colliery, being eminently suitable to be supplied in part by water transport. Here began the notorious Meaford Pound, once detested for its shallowness by all who navigated it, but now appearing to have a somewhat improved depth of water. Along this pound lay the village of Barlaston which once boasted a boatyard. No one knows the name of the boatbuilder who designed the famous 'Barlaston fore-end', a shape of stem widely favoured by Potteries carriers. Its effect was to bring the most forward projecting part of the stempost lower than is found in other designs, and this was thought to make the boats stronger by taking the impact of striking the lock cills off the top bends. The Barlaston fore-end was completely different from that on New Hope, which was built at Rickmansworth. Yet, strangely enough, a motor boat was once built at the latter dock to Rickmansworth design but with the Barlaston bow. She was a motor boat belonging to S.E. Barlow.

Now the fields began to assume the dreary appearance associated with the outskirts of industrial towns, and as *New Hope* approached Sideway Wharf the canal ran above an area of subsidence, its banks being built up by boats owned by the National Coal Board sporting a smart black and white livery. Subsidence of old coal workings produced a landscape of reedy pools, tufty, wiry clumps of grass, and various types of scrub trees, while old spoil heaps were often colonised by birches. To me it was a not unattractive type of scenery, just nature reclaiming her own. Why anyone should think it better to interfere by levelling the ground, sowing grass, planting a few vandal inviting trees, and calling the boring result a Public Open Space is beyond me. Fortunately such concepts were far in the future in 1954, and large areas of these wildernesses were there for those who wished to enjoy them.

The suburbs of Stoke-on-Trent do not extend very far down the low ground of the Trent Valley, and the transition from the landscape of mineral workings to the factories of the Potteries is a sudden one. Hardly had the first factories begun to line the cut than I was again in an area of boats and wharves, approaching my mooring for the night adjacent to the massive Stoke warehouse of the former Anderton Company. I counted nine boats tied up there, some ready to unload into the warehouse in the morning, others bound for one of the nearby private wharves or for Sideway Colliery.

Mersey, Weaver's had taken over the Anderton Company in 1953, and it was to what was now their office at Stoke that I reported in the morning. After the clerk had phoned the head office at Longport, I received orders to go there and load gravel chippings for Manchester. Longport is just under four miles from Stoke and the journey begins by climbing the five locks of the Stoke flight, which take you up past the now demolished rail/canal transhipment warehouse at Stoke station, Cockshute Sidings where a couple of boat youths were busy barrowing flints from a railway wagon into a boat for local delivery, and several well known pottery works to Etruria where, in those days, the top lock still had a canopy over it. Here was a toll office, a maintenance depot and the junction with the Caldon Branch, and above the top lock there was always an evening crowd of tied up boats most of whose cargoes would be destined for local works. It was strange the places that boat people favoured to tie up, for just as Sutton's Stop was the most inconvenient of all the possible tying up places in the Coventry area, so there were several more convenient places in the Potteries than Etruria Top Lock from the point of view of shopping and entertainment. At this hour of the day there were no boats tied up there, though a Mersey, Weaver motor lay on the outside discharging her cargo of soda into the firm's Etruria warehouse.

With deep water under her, *New Hope* set off along the summit; through the heart of Shelton Bar steel works and round its mountainous slag heaps, under dangerously low bridges and past lagoons which had become graveyards for worn out boats, to emerge back in an area of factories near the junction with the Burslem Arm. All around were the bottle-shaped brick kilns for firing the ware, some dead but many still belching black smoke. Now there were wharves again with boats unloading pottery materials at them, the still busy ex Anderton Company boatyard with its unique system of lifting boats out of the water by electric hoist and slings, and finally the gravel loading wharf at Longport with Mersey, Weaver's head office and depot just beyond. I followed two of Mersey, Weaver's own boats, *Eileen* and *Fitton* into the loading length and was completed by 11.30 a.m. The gravel was brought from Trentham by lorry, three lorries being sent, each carrying between six and seven tons. You had to load whatever was in the lorries, in this case a total of 19 tons 12 cwt. However, I was paid the '20 ton minimum' as in the case of Mersey, Weaver's own boatmen, receiving cash in advance which was very pleasing, the rate being 6/9d per ton.

Chapter Five

THE NORTHERN
ROAD AGAIN

•

Ralph Barnett and his family, who worked *Eileen* and *Fitton*, were very friendly and suggested that, as it was Friday, I remain at Longport with them, and that we could all go down together on Saturday to arrive at Trafford Park on Sunday afternoon. The Barnett's worked with their 15 year old son, Roland, and had two younger children, twins, aboard with them. As we gossiped, they told me about their cottage at Rode Heath, and how they hoped to 'drop in' for two loads of flour from Sun Mills on the River Irwell to Burslem Co-op after unloading the chippings. In the course of conversation, Ralph told me how pleased he had been when the firm had finally let him have a motor boat to replace his horse, and how much easier it had been for his wife to look after the children when one or another of them did not have to spend much of the time on the tow-path. *Eileen* was a fine boat, only about 12 years old at the time, and fitted with a two cylinder Gardner engine. With the standard Potteries load of 20 tons apiece, she could drag the *Fitton*, a lightly built Polesworth boat with very sleek lines, along at a great rate.

Before long we were joined by some more boats, which had unloaded that morning, and were to go down to Sideway for coal on the Monday. These were a pair belonging to Potter & Son (Runcorn) Ltd, and a pair of 'Knobsticks' or Anderton Co. boats. Although the Anderton Company had been taken over by Mersey, Weaver, its boats, warehouses and delivery lorries were still administered separately. The old livery was retained too, albeit with a slight alteration to the title, it now being known as the Anderton Carrying Co. Ltd; this being denoted on the cabin sides by a C interspersed between the words Anderton and company. Perhaps their most distinctive feature was the continued use of the 'mileage' method of paying boatmen. This practice had once been almost universal on long distance hauls, but it eventually became superseded by payments based on tonnage to encourage boatmen to put as much weight on their boats as possible. A 20 ton minimum payment was customary where light, bulky cargoes were involved. In practice, however, because of the custom in the Potteries to load 20 tons on each boat, there was no difference in earnings between Mersey, Weaver's tonnage payments and the Anderton Co.'s mileage payments.

The Anderton Company had been one of the oldest undertakings in the canal carrying industry, its predecessor, Alexander Reid & Co., having first put boats on the Weaver in 1829. After a turbulent history as a thorn in the flesh of the Bridgewater Trustees, it had become one of their sub-sidiaries until its sale to the Pamphillon and Boddington familes in 1876. Later it acquired the North Stafford Railway fleet and emerged as the largest carrier in the Potteries trade with, by 1908, some 200 boats regis-tered in Runcorn alone. But now only a handful of boats bore the once familiar black and yellow livery, and the traffic which was once their main-stay, the carriage of crates of china and earthenware, had ceased forever in 1953.

We kicked off at 7.45 a.m. next morning and were soon at the Chatterley end of Harecastle Tunnel. The electrically powered tug which used to drag itself along on a submerged chain, and by which I had been towed through the tunnel on several previous occasions, had gone. Extractor fans had been fitted to ventilate the tunnel and now boats went through under their own power. Given the confined dimensions of the 1½ mile long bore, steering was impossible, so I set the throttle and got down into the cabin where I cooked a hearty breakfast, knowing that there would be little other chance to eat until I tied up that evening. Out in the daylight again, the Barnetts went rapidly ahead, and though they stopped for a while at Rode Heath, were tied up above King's Lock, Middlewich by the time I got down there.

All day long I laboured down the great ladder of locks which lowers the Trent & Mersey to the Cheshire Plain, with only the occasional up-coming boat to make a few ready for me. These locks are very deep and presented difficulties to a single-handed boater working downhill. Once a lock had emptied you had to get the bottom gates open and the boat out so that it could be boarded below the lock, the distance from lock-side to cabin top being too far to jump. This wouldn't have mattered if I could have left the engine ticking over in gear, so that the boat could come out of the cham-ber on its own accord when the gates were opened. But Trent & Mersey locks were peculiar, in that if you tried to do this the boat's stembar would catch behind one gate and make it impossible to open. On some engines forward gear could be engaged by means of a line led out of the engine hole skylight, and left lying on the lock-side, but the National reverse was operated by a wheel, preventing this method from being adopted. My solution was to have a tack-string on the fore-stud, leading back to a conveniently placed stump on the lock-side which would hold the boat, ticking over in gear, an inch or two off the gates. Of course, this could not be secured until the lock was nearly empty, lest the boat catch on the top cill or the line break. With the gates open, the boat would creep out and I could get aboard at the lock tail, but progress was painfully slow and it was eight o'clock in the evening before I tied up below the Big Lock at Middlewich. Not very good going but no doubt I would have discovered some way of speeding things up, had I had the opportunity to work the 'Cheshire Locks' single-handed more regularly.

* * *

Not long ago, after an interval of 36 years, I was able to travel again by boat from the Potteries down to Middlewich. I made this journey on *Sculptor*, Northwich built for the Grand Union Carrying Co. in 1935 and happily preserved form posterity in her Grand Union livery of red, white and blue. In charge of her was Brian Collings, a long time friend and the illustrator of this book. *Sculptor* was doing a promotional tour to advertise English cheese. She was ballasted with coal in bags (for the retail sale of coal and aggregates is now the staple traffic of the remnants of our once great canal carrying industry) topped up with several cardboard cheeses.

It was with great interest that I compared today's canal with that of my youth. Our journey had hardly started when we came across the first major change. Where, in the old days, had stood the Stoke warehouse of the Anderton Company, always with several boats tied up alongside, the canal now twisted and turned through a concrete canyon in the midst of a new urban road network to reach Stoke Bottom Lock; itself a new construction necessitated by the roadworks. It gave me considerable pleasure to reflect that, with the need to reduce carbon dioxide emissions from road transport in order to deal with the threat of global warming, the new road system might well have a much shorter life than the old canal. Above the bottom lock, the canal/railway transhipment warehouse at Stoke station had been demolished, but the site of Cockshute Sidings, albeit now deprived of its rails, was still to be seen.

At the top lock the scene was almost unrecognisable, so much had altered. The removal of wooden canopy which once spanned the lock had perhaps less impact than the strangely suburban atmosphere which had replaced a centre of industry. Gone were the buildings of Wedgwood's works on the towpath side and the wharves and warehouses of the Mersey, Weaver and Anderton companies on the outside had been replaced by prim rows of houses. After halting at the new marina for a visit from the press, and fortifying ourselves at the new pub which is adjacent, we started up again and plunged into the heart of what remains of Shelton Steel Works. Although the blast furnaces and their associated activity had gone, the cut went right through parts of the works still in use, buildings and crane track projecting over the cut just as they had done when L.T.C. Rolt had gone through here in 1939 on that waterway journey so vividly recounted in his book "Narrow Boat".

Had he been with us, Tom Rolt would have been hard put to identify the locations of many of the canalside features of that era. With only a handful of exceptions they had disappeared. The buildings of the Anderton Company's boatyard and its adjacent 1898 warehouse still stood, but we had passed the erstwhile junction of the Burslem Arm with the main line before we realised it, and the eye looked in vain for the Head Office of the Mersey, Weaver and Ship Canal Carrying Co. with its wharf, crane and warehouse at Longport. Tunstall Wharf was still recognisable and the group of boatmen's cottages fronting the towpath nearby was still there.

At the Chatterley end of Harecastle Tunnel we had a wait of about an hour, the last northbound boats of the day being admitted at 2.30 p.m., and we had time to inspect the site of the old Golden Hill ironworks, now just bare ground, and the entrance to the old railway tunnel, the line through which was diverted when it was electrified in the 1960s. The entrance to the original canal tunnel, long disused because of subsidence, had been blocked off from the main canal, but you could still peer inside at about an inch of water covering a thick layer of ochre coloured mud. Eventually we were admitted to the tunnel with two pleasure boats in front and several more behind. Gone were the days of rigging up a plank to protect the forward edge of the engine-hole and then retiring to the cabin while the boat took itself through with the roof skimming the cabin top in places. The towpath had been removed and the roof raised so that now boats could be steered through.

I made myself comfortable on the back beam for the journey through the tunnel and was soon wishing I had put more clothes on, for it became decidedly cold. Not far from the southern entrance of the tunnel can be seen the bricked up entrance to the 'turnrail', a side channel which once gave boats access to the mineral wealth hidden under Harecastle Hill. The presence of iron ore is evident in the colour of the water which enters the tunnel at numerous points. Harecastle Hill is honeycombed with subterranean passages. Apart from those of the railway and canal there is a network of drainage tunnels which, some years ago, were the scene of a particularly unpleasant murder involving the kidnapping of an heiress and her concealment and final demise in this pitch-dark, lonely and frightening place.

Such gloomy recollections were dispelled by the bright afternoon sunshine lighting up the end of our underground journey, and we were soon emerging into the daylight close to Kidsgrove station. Time was when goods were transhipped between canal and rail over the towpath at this point, but the crane which was used in this operation, which had survived until quite recently, has now gone. It is to be feared that the physical remains of our Industrial Revolution will be meagre indeed as we seem to be intent on removing all traces of it. Fortunately there were no modern planners around when Roman aqueducts and Greek temples fell out of use. Kidsgrove used to be a centre of the coal and iron industry and still has the atmosphere of a typical small industrial town of fifty years ago. Here are the first locks of the 16 mile descent to Middlewich, a change of level achieved by 34 deep locks, most of which had been duplicated in the 1830s in order to cope with the heavy traffic. In most places both locks of each pair are still usable, although the interconnecting paddles, designed to save water by using the adjacent lock as a side-pound, were removed after the cessation of commercial traffic.

At the top lock, known to old boatmen as 'Plant's', both locks were still available but, the rest of the way down Cheshire Locks, one lock of each pair had been immobilised by securing the paddle gear with wire. We were told that this was to save water. In fact it had the opposite result, because the tunnel working times produced a lot of downhill boats following one another closely. In the old days the rule was that where locks were close together, the bottom paddles of the upper lock should not be drawn until the top paddles of the lock below had been raised to fill that lock. This prevented a lockfull of water running to waste over the weir. With a long queue of descending pleasure boats, the faster ones, prevented from overtaking by using the duplicate locks, would ignore the old practice, the end result being several boats in one short pound, each one representing the waste of a lockful of water. Not that this meant that anyone got down faster than if they had kept a lock between one boat and the next. Of course, more water could have been saved if the interconnecting paddles which turned one lock into a side-pound of its neighbour had not been removed. I would not advocate that pleasure boaters should be compelled to use these water saving procedures – after all they are on holiday – but there is no reason why they should not be encouraged to do so and thereby, if they wish, get the satisfaction of boating in a professional way. I don't think it is beyond the capability of the average person to operate a side pond or interconnecting paddle, and these should have been left in situ for people to use or not as they wish.

Although we were three-handed our descent of the Cheshire Locks was slow, painfully so it seemed to me, although I gradually became accustomed to the new pace of life on The Cut. Down past Red Bull we went and under the aqueduct which carries the Macclesfield Canal over the Trent & Mersey. The old water tap, noteworthy for its pathetic trickle, which used to be set in the aqueduct wall, had gone. A more noticeable change was the alteration to the passing rule. In my day uphill boats took the towpath side. Now all boats keep to the right.

To me the Trent & Mersey between the tunnel and Middlewich is one of the most interesting parts of the canal system, a string of small industrial settlements now gradually becoming upmarket dormitory villages set in what is sometimes idyllic countryside. L.T.C. Rolt, describing his 1939 voyage in *Cressy* saw things differently and dismissed the long descent of Cheshire Locks in one paragraph. "Not only were the locks very heavy to work, but the surroundings depressing in the extreme – a dreary industrial hinterland that was neither town nor country. The poverty stricken farms and ruined factories of Rode Heath, Hassall Green and Wheelock spoke only too plainly of a rural life transformed by a brief period of industrial expansion, which having laid waste the land and claimed its husbandmen, had passed on to factories new." He was writing, of course, of the pre-war days of agricultural depression, when the countryside would not have looked so prosperous and cared for as it is now. Nevertheless, I think his view was unduly jaundiced, for what could be more pleasant than the tree-lined flight of locks below Red Bull, or the lovely pound between Thurlwood and Hassall Green? Perhaps he descended the Cheshire Locks on one of those rainy days of which this part of the country seems to have more than its fair share.

In the company of several other boats we locked slowly down Red Bull and Lawton locks, with attractive countryside all around and the 1,000ft high summit of Mow Cop looming behind us, discussing our stopping place for the night. Nothing would serve but that we should tie up beside the "Broughton Arms" at Rode Heath, the home of many an old Trent & Mersey boating family. By 7 p.m. we had joined several other boats at this popular mooring and were soon ravenously consuming a pub meal. Here was one thing enjoyed by present day boatmen that had been conspicuously lacking in the 1950s, to wit, cheap and tasty 'Pub Grub', and I reflected upon how nice it would have been, after a hard day's single-handed slogging, to have been able to resort to a pub and have something nice to eat.

It was still early when we had finished our meal and I left my mates tidying up the boat while I had a stroll around the area of meadow and woodland on the towpath side, the meadow here being carefully managed as 'old pasture' in order to preserve its flora and fauna. This pleasant place is, in fact, an area of subsidence caused by brine pumping, the effects of which we were to observe all the way down to Middlewich. It was such a fine evening that we decided that we would walk down to the "Romping Donkey" pub at Hassall Green, two miles down the cut. We had hardly set off along the towpath when we passed the site of Rode Heath Mill, a tall building with an arch under which boats could run to unload and a noted landmark for boatmen in the old days. Like so many other historic canalside buildings it had been demolished, in this case amid much jiggery pokery of listing and de-listing by our so-called Department of the Environment. We may suceed in preserving the canals themselves as strips of water, but we seem intent on destroying everything that gave them interest and meaning, creating instead a Disneyland in which Roses and Castles feature prominently but shafts and shovels do not. To see some more destruction of our waterway heritage one had only to look at the locks we had come down that afternoon, the original paddle gear, perfectly adequate for 200 years, replaced by different designs, the unique centre-paddles with their spindles projecting from the end of the balance beams removed, and a strange policy of putting strapping irons on some top gates and not on others.

Below Rode Heath comes Thurlwood, a place more badly affected than most from subsidence caused by brine pumping, with the result that one of the pair of duplicated locks had to be replaced by a unique steel lock with guillotine gates. This was built in 1958 and demolished in 1987. Old photographs show the whole area of locks and bridges in a very rickety state, just as I remember it in the early 1950s. The bridge and the other lock have both been rebuilt. Thurlwood is notable for the number of houses built facing the canal, these workers cottages now looking distinctly more upmarket than of yore. Below Thurlwood we were in the country again, and a brisk walk of a mile and a half brought us to the "Romping Donkey" at Hassall Green. Here we put the world to rights over a couple of pints before wandering back to our boat. By then it was dark, but this was no problem as the towpath down Cheshire Locks is in exceptionally good condition.

Although it was quite early when we got away the next morning, we found ourselves in a queue of northbound boats making very slow progress. *Sculptor* was ballasted to a draught of 2ft 9ins, but even so, we had no trouble keeping up with the boats in front. There was very little up-coming traffic. At this draught she behaved just like a loaded boat and I found her a pleasure to handle. It was the first time I had ever steered a 'small Northwich', although I did once handle briefly one of the 'big' variety. The Grand Union only had a few small Northwichs built, which was a pity as they were nice looking boats and easy to handle, the only disadvantage being the steel cabins which were cold in winter and hot in summer, and suffered from condensation. It was just as well she was a handy craft as some of the locks coming 'down Cheshire' are awkward to get into.

The pleasantly winding rural pound we had walked along the previous evening took us to Hassall Green again, from where we dropped by many locks, past the hamlet of Malkins Bank to the outskirts of Wheelock. Wheelock's canalside warehouse, still standing, is a sizeable building, reflecting its position as the nearest wharf to Sandbach. In the old days it was a calling point for flyboats. North of the main road bridge at Wheelock the canalside becomes rather unattractive for about threequarters of a mile, after which comes another rural stretch bringing you to the old industrial area of Ettily Heath. Here could be seen the very solid remains of the old North Staffordshire Railway canal transhipment depot, but Murgatroyds Salt works had vanished into the mists of bygone days. There remained another short rural stretch – this canal changes from industrial to rural with amazing felicity – through Stud Green, where subsidence has created an unbelievably skew-whiff house. Beyond here the cut is joined by the main A533 road and runs almost straight for three miles into Middlewich. There is a large modern chemical works along this pound, separated by an extraordinarily difficult bridgehole, its brickwork scarred by many encounters with boats, from the salt works formerly belonging to the Cerebos company. It was here, on a February day in 1950, that John Knill and I had loaded *Columba* with a new traffic, taking salt on a two hundred mile journey to Newbury on the Kennet & Avon Canal.

The approach to Middlewich is characterised by a mile of houses facing the cut but separated from it by the road. In the old days boats could, and did, tie up along here by their family house. Middlewich is still a boatmen's town, and it doesn't take much in the way of enquiry to hear talk of familiar names. It was once a town of tall fuming chimneys which have disappeared with the closure of Seddon's salt works and other firms. Also long gone is the unusual boatmen's toilet between the top and middle locks, a beehive shaped building on the towpath with an earth closet and no door. I had been asked to estimate a time from Rode Heath to Middlewich and had calculated four hours at the most, but it was nearly 2 p.m. when we got to Rumps Lock where three starving boatmen had to tie up and "loose a few by" while we went over the road to the pub, a more down to earth hostelry than those we had visited further up. After a lengthy pause for refreshment we got going only to tie up again above Kings Lock for a press call, giving us an excuse to sample the beer here as well before executing a highly professional turn into the Wardle Cut; and here ended my trip back in time.

* * *

On Sunday morning I got up fairly early and walked back up the locks to help the Barnetts down before setting off round the Big Lock pound. What could be more pleasant than to enjoy the sensation of swinging round bend after tree-shaded bend on that beautiful June morning? The rain which I always associate with that part of the country was unusually absent, there was plenty of water under the boat and the aroma of gently frying bacon rose from the covered frying pan on the range. When the bacon was cooked I drained off the fat, added some tinned tomatoes, and was soon eating from a plate set on the cabin top as I steered with my back against the tiller. Breakfast over I polished the brasswork, and everything was satisfyingly neat and tidy when, cigarette nonchalantly drooping from my lips, I eased off for a handful of empty British Waterways boats waiting orders at Anderton.

A lot of old friends from my days as a mate on the 'Northern Road' had left and there were new faces at Anderton now, but some of the boatmen recognised me. "'Ey-up, there's that young Tommy as used ter work with John Knill. Yo' remember, 'e went in ther Air force. Worro Tom!"

"Worro George, worro Else," I replied, feeling proud as punch as *New Hope* slid majestically past. This was what I had planned for and anticipated for three long years, to be back on the North Western canals with a smart boat among old friends; and it really was as enjoyable in the flesh as it had been in my imagination.

At Barnton Tunnel I discovered that the old system of working through the one-way bore by timetable, had been replaced by traffic lights actuated by the boats. There was no oncoming traffic, so I had a clear run through Barnton, Saltersford and Preston Brook tunnels. At the junction with the Duke's Cut, I stopped to wait for *Eileen* and *Fitton*, so as to hang them on for the 20 mile run along the wide, deep Bridgewater Canal into Manchester. The afternoon passed pleasantly with Ralph and Roland taking turns to join me on *New Hope*, steering while I got a bite to eat, and we were tied up at Trafford Park on the outskirts of Manchester by 7 p.m.

The Trussed Concrete Co.'s wharf was equipped with a grab and this was a place where they didn't hang about. Unloading started at 7.45 a.m. on Monday and was completed within an hour – but you had to keep an eye on the unloaders lest they allowed the grab to damage the boat. Once empty I swept up carefully and made everything tidy before starting up and going round to Hulme Top Lock. Here I reported to a Mr Reynolds, who like me had not been long out of the R.A.F. There was no traffic offering immediately so I settled down to wait. Before long the Barnetts arrived for their orders, departing for Weston Point to load china clay.

There were several old acquaintances tied up at Hulme, including 'Barnton Tommy' Lowe, 'Black Tommy' Lowe and Billy Helm. 'Barnton Tommy', who worked two smart single motors, complained bitterly that the management were insisting on him giving up one motor and having a butty instead. The new policy, I was told, was to cut down on single motors and employ more pairs. To this end, British Waterways were in the process of acquiring some ex British Railways 'station boats' and replacing some of their 9 hp Bolinders with more powerful Listers. Billy Helm, who worked three boats – there were now a number of these 'trebles' operating in the North West, giving rise to some complicated regulations regarding 'taking turn' for loading and discharging – had already lost one of his motors and joined in the lament. There were now no horses to pull boats through the flights of locks at Audlem and Wolverhampton, so boaters were forced to bow-haul empty and work with a long line (five cotton lines spliced together) when loaded. British Waterways even went so far as to convert a couple of single motors into butties.

I also learnt that trade had become much more irregular than it had been three years previously when I had worked in the North West. The imported metal shipments, on which the British Waterways fleet largely relied, had become larger but much more infrequent. Any left over, when all available boats had been loaded, would have been stored to provide boat cargoes between shipments, now it was forwarded immediately by road. This explained management's desire for more butties; the requirement now not being speed, but the ability to assemble the maximum carrying capacity at any one time. They were not wholly successful: the old 'Josher' butties had carried between 24 and 26 tons over the Shropshire Union route, but the newly acquired 'station boats', while being excellent swimmers, were built with a very shallow hold and had very little dry side with 24 tons on board. In addition to these there were two wooden butties built at Rickmansworth in 1952 – the *Aberystwyth* and the *Bangor* – which of course were much larger boats. It is interesting to note that in 1950 the fleet had, in addition to 36 ex 'Josher pups' and three ex Severn & Canal single motors, a number of 'big engines' running about solo. One of these was the *Eagle* which I had worked with Ray White. Others included the *Otter* and the *Avis*. Only about 10 butties were in service then.

On the Wednesday a pair of 'Knobsticks' arrived and, finding that their ship had been delayed, their captain fixed himself up with a cargo of coal for the NCB from Marsland Green on the Bridgewater Canal near Leigh to Runcorn gas works. He suggested that I should do the same, but I rather foolishly didn't take his advice, as I didn't want to get out of turn for a load to Birmingham. I should have realised that when our metal shipment did arrive, it would almost certainly be more than big enough to fill all available boats. I could have done at least one trip to Runcorn and earned much needed cash, but in my ignorance I assumed that I would manage on BW sub-contracts supplemented by the occasional downhill load from the Potteries. In fact, in order to survive in the North West I needed to be aware of every traffic opportunity and to make a wide range of business contacts. There was nearly always somebody somewhere who had work to spare.

In the event it was Friday morning before our group of eight boats were ordered down into the docks to load silicon metal from the SS *Canopus* in No.8 dock. Moreover, loading of the cargo, packed in wooden kegs, didn't get under way until 5.45 p.m. and 45 minutes later the dockers went home for the night. The next morning there was a strong wind blowing, making it difficult to secure *New Hope* alongside the ship single-handed. Loading was completed in half an hour. With her hold full, and an extra tier of barrels on top, she had taken 22 tons.

There was a swing bridge to be negotiated before I got back to Hulme Locks. Lacking any form of horn or siren to attract the bridge-keeper's attention, I was blown over to the side of the channel under the stern of a massive sand barge, before he became aware of my presence and swung the bridge off. Winding in the bottom pound of Hulme so as to avoid a difficult turn at the top, I tied up around noon and went shopping to lay in a sufficient store of food to take me to Birmingham. I had a pleasant surprise at the shop. When it was my turn to be served the shop-keeper enquired if I was 'off the boats', and when I nodded my assent asked me if I would mind waiting while he served the remaining customer. Once the shop was empty he let me have a much greater quantity of rationed items than I was entitled to. After this pleasing episode, I set off for Birmingham in a happy frame of mind.

Once clear of the industry of Manchester, and in the country, the dry windy weather brought a nasty attack of hay-fever which rather spoilt my enjoyment of the deep water of the Bridgewater Canal. Nevertheless, I pressed on to tie up at Anderton at 10 p.m. Next morning I got an early start and made good progress, being pleased to note the enormous improvement to the route, by virtue of the dredging that had been done. I was particularly struck by being able to do the 10 miles from Wardle Lock to Barbridge Junction in 3 ½ hours.

By that evening I had reached the top of 'Drayton and stopped for a meal. But the late June evening was so enticing that I decided to go on. It was a beautiful warm summer's night. The old National was chugging contentedly along and I didn't feel the least bit tired. As lofty valley succeeded dark, wooded 'rocking' I gave myself up to the sheer enjoyment of it all: my smart, deep laden boat, piled high with barrels, responding to the slightest touch of tiller or throttle, making steady, purposeful progress towards her destination.

When I had worked on the Shropshire Union before being called up, I had often laughed at the refusal of some boatmen to work through Grub Street in the dark for fear of ghosts; but I had never worked through there single-handed, and on entering the cutting I experienced a distinct feeling of unease which had nothing to do with the reputation of the place. I sensed danger, a feeling not lessened by having to navigate the narrow places so close to the towpath that anyone – or anything! – could jump aboard. But there was nothing to do but to keep going, with shaft and windlass placed conveniently to hand to repel boarders. Strange it is that I, who have navigated the darkest depths of Birmingham's industrial waterways at night without the slightest qualm, should feel uneasy in the remote depths of rural Staffordshire, and this in the days when car ownership was limited, and the chances of bad characters prowling the countryside were small.

At High Onn, which lay between Gnosall and Wheaton Aston, an old milk churn loading wharf formed a convenient tie-up, and it was here at about 2 a.m. that I decided to stop for a few hours sleep, intending to get away again early. But I had counted without the malevolent heap of old iron in the engine-hole which stubbornly refused duty next morning. I suspected the fuel pump and telephoned the nearby Norbury Depot to seek the assistance of their fitter. He came out to see me but was unable to help, having no knowledge of Nationals. Dismantling the pump, I went over to Tamworth to consult Ted Jones, who advised me to consult C.A.V. in Birmingham. It says much for the efficient public transport of those days that I was able to do this and return to High Onn that evening. The following day I went back to Birmingham, collected the fuel pump, returned to the boat and fitted it, but the engine still stubbornly refused to start.

Next morning, July 2nd, I sent for Ted. He found that the exhaust was choked, new rings were required and the valves needed regrinding. He took the head away to Tamworth and it was not until three days later that he reappeared and reassembled the engine. My log reads:

'Proceeded at 5.45 p.m. Clouds of black smoke and engine started missing. Allowed *Mendip* (now captained by Charlie Atkins) to pass at Brewood and received a tow. Engine worse so stopped near Chillington to examine. Found it difficult to stop engine and impossible to restart. Tow continued to Cut End where tied at 11 p.m.'

The fuel pump being quite clearly at fault, I took it off again and made another trip to Birmingham. This time it was fixed properly and by the afternoon I was going up the 'Twenty-One' like a bat out of hell. I paused quickly at Wolverhampton to replenish the larder then dashed round the 'Hampton Pound in fine style. Down the 'Factory Three' and the Bottom Summit lay in front of me, to be savoured with many a cup of tea and Player's Weights as Sherborne Street drew inexorably nearer. At Spon Lane I spotted a familiar shape in front of me and was glad to be able to give Ray and *Thomas* a tow into Brum. Casting them off at the entrance to the arm, I slunk shamefacedly into the wharf, having taken 9½ days for the journey from Manchester. Ironically, I spent the best part of a day contemplating a succession of lorries which arrived and were unloaded immediately. They spent half an hour unloading *New Hope* at the end of the day, then they didn't start again until five o'clock the next afternoon, this time finishing the job.

I had earned the substantial amount of £18.7.6d (plus about 9/- for working the cargo) for the Manchester trip, but my expectation of some relief to my precarious financial position was dashed when I discovered at Wolverhampton (where Dick Tart was still in charge of Albion Wharf) that, unlike the private carriers who paid spot cash, British Waterways settled with its sub-contractors at the end of the month after the month in which the account was submitted. To make things worse there was no traffic available in Manchester or Weston Point. I rang Fred Woollard the depot superintendent at Worcester, whence shipments to the Midlands were occasionally to be had, without success. Finally, after the weekend, I secured an order from Mersey, Weaver.

My fiancee, Pat, had arranged to spend her holiday aboard, so it was not until her arrival, accompanied by her friend and chaperone, Betty, that we were able to depart. The girls, dressed in holiday finery, were of little help in working the locks, and I was constantly having to grab Betty who seemed determined to get her head knocked off by low bridge-holes. I don't think Pat really enjoyed her holiday, having envisaged a leisurely week of romance, while I was preoccupied with financial worries and wanted to 'get ahead'. We got as far as the "Cross Keys" at Filance that night, just in time for a drink. It was a lovely July evening, indeed it was a week of beautiful weather, and it was a shame that I was unable to relax and enjoy the sort of thing that I had often dreamed about in my long Egyptian exile; boating through the summer countryside in the company of two attractive young ladies. Pat had brought some curtains for the cabin which we rigged up, greatly improving its appearence. The two girls shared the curtained-off crossbed while I slept on the floor. The permissive society had yet to come!

At Stoke I received orders to load at Sideway Colliery for Henry Seddons & Sons' salt works at Middlewich. Here the coal was loaded into the boat from a conveyor belt which ran under the main line railway separating the colliery from the cut. The proceedings were quite fast and only moderately dusty. With just under 20 tons on board we set off, the girls mopping and polishing, up the five locks at Stoke and round the summit. At Longport we stopped to collect the ticket and money which was 4/1d per ton, 20 tons minimum, cash in advance. I was directed to the former Anderton Company's office. Mersey, Weaver had never entirely integrated the Anderton Company into its organisation and tended to operate as though there were two separate firms. The Seddons coal job was an ex Anderton Company contract. I discovered the office behind the boatyard where a large cobbled courtyard was ranged about by extensive stabling, a reminder of the days when the Anderton Company was a power in the transport world. Starting again, we carried on through Harecastle Tunnel and down to Church Lawton where we tied up on another beautiful evening. Romance was in the air, but I was very tired and did not in the least feel like sitting on the stone steps of the lock watching the sunset.

At half past four next morning I was on my way through a heavy mist promising hot weather to come. My companions were still in bed, if not actually slumbering, as a motor boat's cabin is very noisy with the engine running. We arrived at the salt works at lunchtime. Immediately a gang of men fell on the coal and we were emptied in short order. I was pleasantly surprised to get 5/- 'sweeping up money'.

There were no orders at Anderton. The girls went home from Northwich station and I was left to bite my nails and count the coppers for the next ten days. I had one little job in the meantime, towing two empty Seddon's boats to Middlewich, but it was hardly worth the 10/- payment. Looking back, I find it difficult to explain why, when no B.W. orders were forthcoming, I didn't apply to Mersey, Weaver – who had a branch office at Anderton – for a load.

Eventually the boats waiting at Anderton were ordered down to Weston Point and *New Hope* was loaded with 22 tons of spelter overside from a flat. I worked back up the Weaver, intending to spend the night below the Lift, but just below Acton Bridge there came a clatter from the engine hole, followed by a tremendous bang. Hastening along the gunwhale, and peering in through the engine hole doors, I was horrified by the chaos within. There was a hole in the side of the engine and bits of metal all over the floor. The engine had 'shoved a leg out'; in other words the connecting rod had come adrift and broken out of the cast iron casing. My National, whose infuriating unreliability I had endured for the past two months, was a complete write-off.

There was nothing to do but to put plenty of ropes out and to telephone British Waterways from the swing bridge cabin. Next morning a tow materialised in the shape of Freddie Morton with the *Parrot* and Ronnie Saxon with the *Chub*. When we got above the Lift we found the BW fleet superintendent waiting, and it was arranged that Fred should tow me to Birmingham, no charge being made for this service. We got away at noon and tied up at Nantwich just after midnight. I had some doubts as to whether it would be possible to steer *New Hope* under tow, but she steered almost as easily as a butty and we made very good time.

Next morning we managed to produce five cotton lines between us and spliced them together to make a long line for working up Audlem Locks. Such an operation was entirely new to me. When I had worked this route in 1950 it had been possible to hire a horse to pull butties through the flight. The principle of working five lines was to keep 'a lock between'. In other words the butty is separated from the motor by an intermediate lock, thus enabling the boats to work almost as fast as a single motor. All the spare line was kept on the motor's counter so that the motor steerer could adjust the length as required. The locks were against us, so that as soon as I had got *New Hope* in one lock, shut the gates and drawn the paddles, I would run up to the next lock. *Parrot* would be in this one, which by then would nearly be full. I would start *Parrot* ahead as Fred returned from emptying the next lock. I shut the top gates behind him and drew a bottom paddle, then ran back down to board *New Hope* – by then nearly ready to leave the lock – and got ready to steer up the pound as the line tautened from *Parrot*. This was the stage at which there would be 'a lock between'. The long line was used similarly at the Adderley and Drayton flights, and the speed at which we worked can be judged by our arrival at Norbury at 9.30 p.m., 13 ½ hours after leaving Nantwich; very respectable timing for a two-handed pair.

The following night saw us at Wolverhampton and we arrived in Birmingham by noon the next day. I had been so preoccupied with the journey that my predicament had not really had time to sink in. But once I had tied up at Sherborne Street the situation hit me with full force. I was practically penniless and had a boat with no engine. All my carefully laid plans, backed by the savings acquired by three years of pinching and scraping had been brought to nothing. There was only one person to consult and that was John Knill. After several exchanges by telephone a ray of light began to dawn on the situation. We had discussed the question of insurance when I had been getting *New Hope* ready, and had agreed on the same policy which he had, one which included both engine breakdown and loss of earnings cover. I had a vague idea that I had left the arrangements in his hands, and was absolutely certain that I had neither signed a proposal nor paid a premium. The whole affair is still puzzling to me but it eventually transpired that I was indeed covered.

The next thing was to discuss possible engines. I fancied one of the 9 hp Bolinders which B.W. was then removing from some of its Northern boats. John tried hard to persuade me to have the twin cylinder semi-diesel Bolinder which he had used for a short time in *Columba*. It was almost new, but I knew the difficulties he had had with it – it was 'a cow' to start – and I positively refused to have anything to do with it. I don't know where it ended up, but eventually it was decided that a Ruston engine which had been taken out of Barlow's *Cairo* would suit me.

I had done a trip or two with George Smith on *Cairo* and remembered how he had liked the engine. It was only about six years old, but although it ran perfectly in day to day use, it was prone to excessive wear on the main bearings, due – it is now thought – to it being designed for use a stationary engine. I wasn't too bothered about this, after all I was getting it for nothing, and it was not going to be belted up and down 'The Junction' towing a butty week after week as it had been in Barlow's service. On the rest of the canal system the cuts were so shallow, that most of the time it was impossible to use more than a fraction of the power of an engine of this size.

For some reason, goodness knows why, it was decided to tow *New Hope* to Tardebigge to have the old engine removed by the yard crane, though there were plenty of nearby places where this could have been done. Having arrived there and removed the National, which was promptly taken away by the insurance company, there was then an interminable delay while they arranged the purchase and installation of the new engine.

CHAPTER SIX

THE OLD CUT

·

With the engine removed I was presented with a golden opportunity to clean the engine-hole bilges, plenty of sawdust being available from the carpenter's shop. After this had been done I was at a loose end, so I passed the time 'hobbling' for boats going up and down the long flight of thirty locks at Tardebigge, or making an occasional trip out to Cannock or down to Worcester with Ray. It was on one of these trips that I jumped in the cut at Bromford Stop. *Thomas* was always gauged there, and I stepped ashore as usual, to check the boat with the strap. Suddenly I found myself sliding, hobnail boots on slippery blue brick, towards the cut. It was only seven feet wide at the stop place, so I flung myself as far over towards the other side as I could, heaving myself on to the island with only the lower part of my body getting wet. Unfortunately my cigarettes were in my trouser pocket and were rendered completely unsmokeable. I shall never forget the look on the toll clerk's face as he stepped out of the office just in time to see the performance.

Falling in the cut was nothing unusual for me. Once, steering *Thomas* into one of the Tardebigge locks, I stepped ashore, short shaft in hand ready to use it to push shut the inside bottom gate. Clumsily I managed to get the shaft across the walls on each side of the steps with the inevitable result!

During these journeys up and down the 'Worcester Cut' I was introduced to many of the tricks boatmen played on one another. There was a constant war, with rapidly shifting alliances, between Ray and his mate Muriel – a lady of uncertain temper – and the other boatmen, lock-keepers, tug-men, and the unfortunate section inspector who was the local representative of authority. When *Thomas* was being towed through Wast Hill Tunnel, Muriel would sprinkle the fire with water (some alleged it was pee) creating an inpenetrable smog through which the tugmen had to grope on their return journey. Following motor boats would be prevented from overtaking by dint of dropping a bundle of baling wire in a convenient bridge-hole for them to pick up on their blades. When pulling the boat through 'Dennister' (Dunhampstead) Tunnel I was always warned to watch out for razor blades inserted behind the handrail, though personally I thankfully never had a painful encounter with one.

In one of the canalside houses at Tardebigge lived a lady who was reputed to spend much of her time at her bathroom window spying on boatmen coming up the locks. One day, as *Thomas* was being tied up at the wharf, she materialised and accused Ray of kicking the horse. This was nonsense as he never wore anything other than plimsoles at work, regardless of the weather. When Muriel heard about this she went to the house and banged on the door. The woman opened it.

"We aren't all deaf you know."

"You will be when I've finished with you!"

A classic start to a typical canalside slanging match, which was only prevented from developing into a fight by the arrival of a gentleman who claimed to be a special constable.

Other canalside conversations were on a lighter note. A woman on a boat in the drydock was invited ashore by one of her mates.

"I can't, I haven't any knickers to wear."

(There were men working in the dock who would certainly look up as she walked the plank between boat and shore)

"Why haven't you got any?"

"They're in the wash."

"Why don't you have two pairs?"

With a hint of impatience:

"I can't wear more than one pair at once can I!"

There was one person of whom Muriel was in awe and that was Fanny Ballinger. Charlie was an easy going old gentleman but his wife, always immaculately dressed and coiffeured, ruled the boatmen with a rod of iron. When matters were not going to her liking she was wont to enquire: "Why don't you take the fiddling boats to Wainlodes Hill (a well known boat graveyard) Charlie?"

Ray, always a coiner of catch-phrases, was fond of doing a credible imitation of his boss's wife saying this. But his favourite expression, uttered on every possible occasion, was: "So what? The cut's open all night!" This had its origin in an argument with the section inspector over the absence of staff after 5 p.m. to deal with the empty pounds often encountered. Complaining about the delay, he was told that he could easily catch up lost time as the canal was open all night. Thereafter, if any of the lock-keepers objected to *Thomas* going through in the middle of the night, the favourite phrase was pronounced with relish. Ray was one of the great eccentrics of the 1950s canal boating scene and his death, in 1987, was a great loss.

Life was far from dull at Tardebigge, but I fretted and fumed as week followed week with no development engine-wise. The Ruston was sent to Ted Jones for overhaul. After all it was only fair he should have his 'insurance job' as he had been so accommodating about my repairs bill. Ted insisted upon the boat being taken to Glascote for installation to take place. The Tardebigge tug towed me through the tunnels as far as the paper mills at Lifford, where I was picked up by a Cresswell's tug on its way back to Sandwell Colliery and taken to Farmer's Bridge. There I was met by Ted's assistant, Pete, who helped me to bow-haul down 'The Thirteen' and 'The Eleven' to Salford Junction. T & S Element, who had a depot at Salford Bridge, were to tow me to Glascote.

Next morning I hooked on to one of their horse-drawn Joey boats bound for Pooley Hall Colliery in charge of 'Cakey Bill' Stevens, their wharf foreman. To tow two empty boats behind a horse requires a complicated arrangement of ropes. One rope goes from the stern of the leading boat to the mast beam of the following vessel, while another connects the stern beam of the leading boat to the fore-end stud of that in the rear. In true Joey boat fashion we stopped for a mid-day pint below Minworth, arriving at Glascote in the afternoon.

While the engine was being installed, I was contacted by George Element, who was in charge of the boat side of the business at Salford Bridge. There was another depot at Oldbury where the boats were run by Sam Element. It was suggested that when *New Hope* was ready for work, I should load at Pooley for the G.E.C. works at Witton. Thus it came about that, on the 18th November 1954, I found myself under the chute at Pooley loading 17 tons and 12 cwt of pea slack. Because *New Hope* had not been loaded for several months, I deliberately loaded her lightly in case she had dried out enough to make her leak. It was a good job that I did so because, being unacquainted with the route, it never occurred to me that it was too shallow to be navigated with the sort of load carried on the adjacent canals; the Birmingham & Fazeley was, after all, in regular daily use by loaded boats.

Having tidied up and mopped off all the coal dust, I left Pooley basin, glad to be back at work. No one could have been happier as, with a steaming cup of tea in front of me, I steered through the winter dusk, to tie up at Glascote an hour later. The following day another 7 ½ hours boating brought me to Witton. After discharging at the G.E.C., I tied up at Salford Bridge Wharf and went to see George Element, who asked me if I would be interested in carrying to Witton regularly and at what rate. I didn't know that local carrying around Birmingham commanded a much higher rate than journeys of a similar length elsewhere. However, I knew that being the only cabin-boat on the job, and therefore having priority over the Joey boats for unloading, I could do three trips a week; and having had no undue trouble with my cargo, assumed that I should be able to carry at least 20 tons per trip. The only comparable job I knew of was that from Pooley to Longford Power Station for which sub-contractors were paid 3/6d per ton. I therefore suggested a rate of 4/-. George was horrified: "You can't make it pay at that rate!" he said, and so we fixed on 5/-. The resulting weekly income compared very favourably with any other carrying job that I knew of. Mulling over these matters on the way back to Pooley, I envisaged a very rosy future. However all that glitters is not gold, and I was to find out that there were reasons why this particular gold mine was not already being thoroughly exploited.

The second trip that I made from Pooley to Witton was fraught with difficulty. With 18 tons and 15 cwt of slack, *New Hope* ran aground in three bridge-holes before reaching Amington where I had to stop to fix the water pump. I also ran aground below the first two locks of the Curdworth flight and had to stop to remove baling wire and tyres from the propellor. It was 5.15 p.m. when I tied up (in the middle of the cut) at Bodymoor Heath, having taken six hours for a journey normally occupying only three. The following day it took me a further five and a half hours to reach Witton after being stuck for a considerable time at Minworth Bottom Lock and picking up lots of rubbish on the blades en route.

On my third trip I tied up at the G.E.C. late on a Friday afternoon. With some spending money now in my pocket, I had a wash and change and set out for a stroll through this unfamiliar part of the town in the direction of the city. Along the Lichfield Road, crowded with Friday night shoppers, lamplight spilled over the outside displays of late closing ironmongers and greengrocers. At Aston Cross I came across a cafe and went in for a cup of tea and a meal, followed by a couple of hours at the pictures. Emerging into a mild, early winter night, I refreshed myself with a pint of beer at one of Aston's numerous pubs before strolling back towards Salford Bridge. A train hooted mournfully as it rumbled across the bridge by Aston station, and in the dark shadows underneath, a short skirted girl whispered an invitation. I felt happy and content to be back in Birmingham with my engine troubles over and plenty of well paying work in prospect.

The next two trips were not too difficult and so it was arranged that I should try towing an Element open boat. Elements provided the boatman and paid me £3 a trip for towage. The first boatman I had was Albert Rookes who, though he was only 15, was an expert. Albert had been taught the trade by a character known as 'Old Clogs', and he was fond of remarking to the other youths who worked for Elements that nobody could possibly know anything about boating unless they had worked with Clogs. The experiment was not very successful and was discontinued at the end of December. It had been very hard work, not only because of the bad condition of the cut, but because the locks were inconveniently laid out for working a pair of boats. Where locks were arranged close together in flights, the motor and its butty could proceed independently. The steerer of the motor would start each lock filling or emptying behind him, so when the butty reached it all the bow-hauler had to do was to open the gates. Under favourable conditions the butty could virtually keep time with the motor and there would be little delay. But on the Old Cut most locks were so widely separated that the butty had to be towed through each pound.

The round trip took about twenty hours of boating to which must be added the time spent loading and unloading. Long hours were not the only problem: in order to accommodate working hours at both the colliery and the G.E.C. (the latter would rarely empty boats after 2 p.m.) it was preferable to work from the Tamworth end of the canal in order to be sure of an early arrival at Witton on alternate days. The boatmen who were working with me, Albert being followed by another young Birmingham-Irish lad, Michael Cusack, lived in the Nechells area of Birmingham and, naturally not only expected to spend every other evening at home, but also to finish the week's work by Saturday mid-day. Personally, although two trips a week with a pair earned me about the same amount as three with a single motor, there was no advantage as far as hours worked were concerned; whilst towing made life a lot more difficult, especially in very bad weather.

When it became apparent that I could only get loads of about 18 tons up the Old Cut the rate was increased to 5/6d per ton. When the towing finished I adopted the practice of working from Salford Bridge end, leaving early on alternate days and spending the night at 'The Dog' at Bodymoor Heath or 'The Bakehouse' at Curdworth. Getting up at about six or seven in the morning, the first task was to light the primus for a pot of tea, the essential preliminary to starting work. If it was cold weather this would be laced with a drop of rum. The fire in the cabin range would then

Plum Pudding tunnel on the 'North Stafford'.

Night working in a 'Shroppie Rockin'.

be lit using plenty of paraffin, so that when I slid back the slide and looked out, I would see flames coming out of the chimney, a cheering sight on an unpleasant winter morning. *New Hope*'s Ruston engine was peculiar in that the starting handle had to be swung anti-clockwise, and the only way to operate the decompression lever was to tie a piece of string to it, securing the other end in such a way that I could jerk it from where I stood to swing the engine. It wasn't long, though, before I learnt to manage without the decompression lever and to start the engine by bouncing it against the compression and forcing it over compression on the rebound. Unlike a National, it could always be relied on to start.

In winter, of course, it was dark at that time in the morning, and though *New Hope* had no headlight, the lights of the city, reflected from the sky, gave ample visibility. Approaching Minworth Top Lock the canal ran alongside the Kingsbury Road and boatmen would be dazzled by the lights of oncoming cars. This was also a bad place for floating rubbish which had to be removed before the top gate could be opened. It was rare to have any locks ready on the downhill journey because of the preponderance of downhill boats. Only a few locks were close enough together to enable a single-handed boatman to leave his boat in one lock while going forward to fill the next. Most of the time there was a tiresome routine of stopping above the lock, filling it, getting back on the boat, driving it in, stopping it by strapping the gate, emptying the lock and steering down to the next, where the whole procedure would be repeated, often to the accompaniment of gale force winds, rain or snow. The bottom of Curdworth Locks, four hours out of Salford Bridge, signalled breakfast time. If weather permitted this would be eaten while steering down the long straight pound to Fazeley Junction, otherwise I would pause in the bottom lock for a few minutes. The remainder of the journey to Pooley took about two hours.

After loading I would mop off and generally tidy the boat. On other runs where the loading arrangements allowed the stands to remain in position, I would put up the deckboard and planks, making sure they were straight and level as the appearance of a loaded boat was improved by doing this. While I was trading to Witton – unloading three times a week and having to remove everything from the hold on each occasion – I soon removed the mast, deckboard and stands and left them ashore to make life a bit easier. I then only had to remove the beams and unscrew the bracing chains when unloading. The coal had to be kept towards the middle of the boat as much as possible because the G.E.C. grab was too big to work in front of the mast.

Apart from a couple of short stretches where mining subsidence had resulted in deep water, the cut between Pooley and Fazeley was slow going. The sharp turn before the river Tame aqueduct was particularly difficult to negotiate. From Fazeley to Curdworth Bottom Lock there was ample water, the three miles being covered in an hour, but it was at this lock that the real trouble began. The flush of water caused by emptying locks usually ensured that the lock tails were kept clear of mud. Not so on the Old Cut, where there was a hump of mud and debris about forty feet below each lock in what was sometimes an otherwise deep pound. Some of these scours were worse than others, that below Common Lock being the worst. Aground on one, the single-handed boatman was helpless, being unable to get ashore. If he had been able to – leaving the engine in gear – he could have drawn a flush (by quickly opening and closing the paddles) to lift the boat enough for it to creep into the lock. Going astern and taking a series of runs at a scour sometimes worked, but usually only resulted in a bladeful of rubbish. On one occasion I picked up a complete set of bedsprings in the chamber of Curdworth Bottom Lock. As this place was completely isolated, except for the lockside 'company' houses, I speculated somewhat ruefully as to where it had come from.

The 'Company's Men', or British Waterways employees, were not always helpful. One afternoon, firmly stuck below Common Lock, one of them hove into sight along the towpath. I asked him to draw me a flush. "I'm a lengthman, not a lock-keeper," he retorted and cycled off, quite unconcerned about the toll paying traffic whence came his pay packet. Eventually, having been obliged to winch *New Hope* into Common Lock on a couple of occasions, B.W. hired a privately owned spoon dredger and removed the worst of the scours. Unbelievably, Fazeley maintenance yard had no dredging equipment whatsoever. The scours soon returned however, and anyone going up Curdworth Locks today can see evidence of dredging below many of the locks. I have often wondered why these scours should have formed without any apparent reason, and speculated as to whether downhill loaded traffic – which had ended early in the 1950s – would have prevented them from forming.

The locks on the Old Cut, besides being awkwardly sited, were also rather short. At 71ft 3ins, *New Hope* was not an exceptionally long boat, but I had to remove several fenders in order to be able to close or open the single leaf bottom gates. Even then it was sometimes necessary to turn the 'elum' and put the engine in reverse in order to get clearance to open the bottom gates when going downhill. Being unable to carry the necessary number of stern fenders meant that the rudder and tiller were unprotected from accidental contact with cills and gates. Fortunately it was possible to work the locks in the normal way when going uphill. My routine was to step off the boat at the tail of the lock, and draw a bit of top paddle to stop the boat before it hit the cill, effectively holding the boat up to the cill at the same time. The amount of paddle and its timing had to be nicely judged or the boat would hit the cill or be washed back out of the chamber. This done, I would tear down to the bottom gate, shut it and race back up to the top and draw the other paddles.

Above Curdworth Locks was a shallow pound which included the short and narrow 'Paddy's Tunnel'. This caused me no problems when I started to trade on the canal, but it gradually became full of mud. Eventually *New Hope* had extreme difficulty negotiating it, and did so slowly and painfully to the accompaniment of clouds of black smoke caused by the propellor working in a mixture of mud and dead leaves. The way of dealing with a confined space like this tunnel, was to dredge a hole at each end and let the passage of boats push the mud out of the tunnel and into the holes, but repeated complaints failed to get B.W. to take any action.

The next black spot was Minworth Bottom Lock, the bridge below which was frequently full of rubbish. Above Minworth Locks the 'Four Mile' pound would not have been so bad, except for similarly choked bridgeholes. The canal was not terribly deep, except for the length between Butlers and Holly Lane bridges, where the boat flew along so fast that I was prompted to measure the depth and found no less than five feet of water! Why this one short bridge's length should have been so deep is a mystery. Grand Union boatmen referred to this place as 'The Pictures', and would sometimes tie up there adjacent to the factory of Constructors Limited, to which I sometimes took a load from Saltley Sidings, whilst visiting the local flea pit. It was possible to get stuck in several of the bridges on the 'Four Mile', and the only thing to do was to take repeated runs at the bridge-hole until you forced a way through. The obstructions were old bedsteads, bikes, oil drums and similar articles. Bridges were always entered at a snail's pace, but if you hit an obstacle between bridges when travelling rather faster it would cause a nasty jar and sometimes make the boat heel over. This was known as 'hitting a rough 'un'.

Near Bromford the Birlec factory spanned the canal for a considerable distance. One evening, coming up loaded, I ran into an obstruction here right in the middle of the cut. Although the boat would move pivot-wise, all my efforts to get it off were in vain, so I had to spend the night in this insalubrious place. Early next morning the flush of water from an approaching Grand Union pair, going empty round to the collieries, lifted me clear. The boatman was not very pleased, thinking that I had decided

to spend the night in the shelter of the factory without tying up, a danger-
ous thing to do, as it would have been difficult to see *New Hope* in the
gloom with the view ahead restricted by the high bows and cratch of an
empty boat. After 'The Birlec', Trout Pool Bridge – notorious for the varied collection of ironmongery lurking in its shallows – was the last obstacle
before reaching G.E.C.

The G.E.C., whose unloading length was immediately below the bottom
lock of the Perry Barr flight on the Tame Valley Canal, was equipped with
a very large grab which, unlike many others on the canals, was kind to
your false floors. Boats were moved backwards and forwards under it by
two capstans with hooks on the end of their ropes, and unloading was
quick and convenient though apt to be more or less dusty depending on
the strength of the wind. There was always a crowd of Joey boats here waiting emptying, some of which had come up the Old Cut and others which
had been loaded at Saltley Sidings. There was no winding hole at Witton
so the half mile back to Salford Junction had to be covered in reverse.

A feature of the Old Cut was its general air of dreariness, commented
on by both Eily Gayford and Emma Smith in their books on wartime boating. Certainly I found the Pooley to Witton run to be the most depressing
I experienced in my boating career. The first few miles out from Salford
Junction were lined by unlovely inter-war factories, the rest of the way as
far as Fazeley running through a landscape of soggy, level fields. Despite
this, however, it was hard to put a finger on exactly why this canal was so
unlikeable. The explanation must lie in the fact that each canal has its
own individual atmosphere not necessarily related to scenery or surroundings.

CHAPTER SEVEN

SALFORD BRIDGE

Development of the Gravelly Hill area of Birmingham started in the early 1900s and the point where the Lichfield Road crosses the canal at Salford Bridge was an obvious strategic point, first for the delivery of building materials and later for the supply of coal to the surrounding district. By 1904 it was sufficiently well developed to justify extention of the electric tramway from the previous terminus at Aston Cross.

There were two wharves at Salford Bridge, one on the Tame Valley Canal with access from Leamington Road, and one on the other side of the bridge beside the Birmingham & Fazeley Canal. In 1954 both these wharves were occupied by Messrs T & S Element, one of the largest carriers and contractors on the B.C.N. A couple of years previously there had also been an adjacent boatyard belonging to Spencer, Abbott but this firm of coal factors no longer owned any boats and its new lorries could be seen parked on the central reservation – once used by the city's trams – of the Tyburn Road.

The Leamington Road wharf, always known as the 'boat' wharf to distinguish it from the other which was called the 'lorry' wharf, was entered through an unobtrusive cobbled archway which linked the foreman's house and a block of stables. The foreman at this time was Mr W. Stevens, known to all as 'Cakey Bill' because of his fondness for confectionery. His father had worked for Elements, and his son, also known as Bill, still did so. There was a row of houses in Leamington Road whose yard gates opened out onto the wharf. These were mostly occupied by serving and retired employees. The wharf was no longer used for unloading coal, but was usually lined with loaded or empty Joey boats, often tied two abreast, waiting to start or continue their journeys.

The foreman's job was to look after the horses, and when not engaged in this he would be out doing a bit of boating or unloading a boat. There were about ten horses kept at Salford Bridge, but Elements also had a large establishment at Ormond Street, Aston, where there was a stock of horses used for railway cartage. Elements had a good relationship with the London Midland Region of British Railways. Ormond Street was looked after by an old character called 'Lion-tamer', so called because he was fond of saying that man was made to tame lions, not horses.

Because it was not the custom for the local traffic to work on Sundays, this was the day when the horses were shod by a visiting farrier who brought all his equipment with him. There was a large pile of used straw and manure which was removed every now and then by lorry – in the old days it would have been boated out into the country for use on some farmer's fields. There was always something going on at the wharf, boat-men bringing their horses into the stables or taking them out, horseshoes striking sparks from the cobbles, a boat being tied up, passing canal traffic, or more to the interest of lusty boat youths, the women who used the towpath as a short cut to their work at the G.E.C.

The lorry wharf on the other side of the bridge held a small stock of house coal, a garage for the lorries (only a handful were kept here) and the company's office, a modern building whose windows commanded a fine view of the junction. To stand here and watch the canal traffic was fascinating and it was rarely necessary to wait long to see a boat. Besides the traffic coming up the Old Cut, there were coal boats from Walsall Wood and from the collieries on Cannock Chase, other coal boats that had loaded at the nearby Saltley Sidings, cargoes of rubbish, and 'black boats' used in the short distance tar trade from local gasworks to the tar distillery at Oldbury. These were interspersed with occasional Thos. Clayton motor boats, but the finest sight of all was to watch a horse-drawn Clayton cabin boat, in all the glory of its traditional style crimson livery, agleam with shining brasswork and deep laden with its aromatic cargo of tar, take the 45 degree turn between the Warwick & Birmingham Junction Canal and the Birmingham & Fazeley in the direction of Aston. Heeling over to the pull of the horse, the steerer, often a lady of advanced years, would be rowing frantically at the tiller so as to put her charge neatly into the narrow stop place. Long distance craft were represented by empty pairs of British Waterways boats working through from the wharves at Tyseley, Camp Hill or Fazeley Street to the Warwickshire collieries.

On the opposite bank from Elements, in the angle between the Warwick & Birmingham and Birmingham & Fazeley as it headed towards the city centre, stood Salford Junction toll office whose clerk had a busy time gauging boats in the three separate stop places radiating from the junction, that on the Tame Valley Canal being on the far side of Salford Bridge.

This office was to be closed within a short time, the work of gauging boats and issuing tickets being either undertaken elsewhere or foregone in favour of declarations from the carriers and collieries.

The *genius locii* of Salford Bridge was George Element, a genial, portly and bespectacled figure who appeared on the boat wharf sharp at seven each morning. His was the second generation of Element's since the founding of the firm. One of the original founders, old Tom Element, occasionally swept on to the wharf in a huge black chauffeur-driven car. Everyone held him in great awe and he rarely spoke to anyone except his sons and nephews. In contrast, George was addressed by his christian name by even the youngest employee. If any boats had not departed by 7 a.m. he would make remarks about 'working office hours' and his favourite expletive was 'Gor Blimey!' pronounced in a strong Birmingham accent. He was not the slightest bit put out to find, as frequently happened, that one of the boat kids had overslept, and would drive round to the offender's house and get him out of bed. George was universally popular and the firm paid good wages slightly over the union rate. Elements had probably the best maintained fleet of Joey boats on the B.C.N. Here were no ancient leaky wrecks, but good dry boats with a roomy cabin in which it was no hardship to spend a night aboard if necessary.

Three other members of the Element family occupied the office besides George. One – a brother I think – was in charge of the lorries and house coal sales, then there was Stan Element who kept the accounts, and also someone's daughter or niece; I never did sort out the ramifications of the whole family. The firm had another depot at Oldbury from which the tug service to Cannock Chase and 'Upper' Birmingham was operated. The tug captain rejoiced in the name of 'Yampy Tom'. The Oldbury office was presided over by Sam Element (who I think was George's cousin) assisted by 'Cooksy', an old retainer who occupied a similar position to 'Cakey Bill' at Salford Bridge.

Elements had three horses regularly engaged on the Pooley Hall to G.E.C. traffic, supplemented by extra trips as men and horses were available. This type of traffic was always quantified in terms of horses rather than boats because the system of changing boats at each end – instead of waiting to load and unload as was done in the long distance trade – meant that there were far more boats than horses or sets of men working on the canal. There were no captains or mates in the Joey boat system of working. Each boat was worked by a horseman and a boatman, both of whom were paid at the same rate. On the long distance trade, only the captain was usually employed and he had to find and pay the mate himself. In practice the roles of horseman and boatman were interchangeable, and because it was nearly always the case that one of the crew was older and more experienced than the other, he would be tacitly regarded as being in charge.

The standard amount of work per week was four round trips between Pooley and Witton, but there were a number of old men and kids on the job who were allowed to do only three trips if they wished. The rate of remunneration was £2.2s per trip. Boats doing four trips left Salford Bridge on Mondays, changed to a loaded boat at Pooley and returned as far as 'The Bakehouse' in the pound above Curdworth Locks. On Tuesday they would proceed to Witton, change boats, return to Pooley and get back as far as "The Park" public house below Glascote Locks. An early start on the Wednesday would take them in to Witton where they changed boats again, but this time finishing early, if everything went according to plan by 1 p.m. The whole routine would then be repeated between Thursday and Saturday.

Boats doing three trips started from Salford Bridge on Monday, Wednesday and Friday, changed at Pooley and came back to "The Dog" at Bodymoor Heath. On Tuesday, Thursday and Saturday they would proceed to Witton, change boats and tie up at Salford Bridge around mid-day. It can be seen that this pattern allowed three afternoons off in a six day week. Sometimes the men would spend a free afternoon loading a boat at Saltley Sidings for which they received a shilling for every ton. "The Dog" was a remote and inaccessible place and boatmen always spent the night on board when tied up there. It was possible to get home by bus from 'The Bakehouse', or even from "The Park"; but an extra night at home would have to be set against getting up earlier the following morning, though the first buses ran quite early in those days.

Besides Elements, S.E. Barlow operated some Joey boats on the Old Cut. They traded between Baddesley Colliery near Atherstone and J. Wrights in the second pound of Aston Locks, and between Pooley Hall Colliery and the Science Museum, whose wharf was located on the Whitmore Arm in the Thirteen. Their boats also served two wharves belonging to J. Parkes at Aston, known to boatmen as Upper and Lower Parkes's.

A Joey boat was just a bare hull and cabin, everything moveable went with a set of men and had to be changed over from a loaded to an empty boat and vice versa. The inventory of equipment was long and is worth listing.

MAST: for which a gap was left between the forward and middle of the three 'rucks' of coal; this being the method of loading a Joey boat, leaving a gap so that the mast step was accessible and also providing a 'lade-hole' where water could be scooped out. The mast was secured to the mast beam by a length of chain. It was rigged vertically in a loaded boat and in a slanting fashion on an empty one, so as to clear low bridges, not being telescopic as was the mast of a cabin boat.

TOWLINE: a six pound cotton line.

BLOCK: a pulley attached to the mast for use when starting a loaded boat out of a lock.

SHAFTS: a 'long' one and a shorter 'cabin' one.

'ELUM: or rudder. This was smaller and lighter than the cabin boat equivalent and the bottom 'iron' was moveable. To rig the 'elum' the top iron was engaged in its hole at the top of the stern post, the bottom iron was raised and lined up with the bottom cup and then pushed down into place with the cabin shaft. The 'elum' carried a short length of line to enable it to be pulled round to clear the cill in a short lock.

TILLER: this was removable and would, of course, be attached to the 'elum'.

STRAP: for stopping the boat and shutting the gate in a downhill lock.

TACK STRING: a length of cotton line put to various uses including acting as a block rope. There were no tying up ropes on Joey boats which were secured by a chain wrapped round the middle beam; shore chains were provided at well used wharves.

CABIN STOVE: with collar and chimney. All three were transferred from one boat to another, an unpleasant job as the stove would still have some fire in it, though it was allowed to die down before changing.

When a boat with her 'tools' on board was left unattended, everything portable was put in the cabin which was secured by bolting down the slide and securing the doors with a locking bar and padlock. Boats that did not have their tools on board couldn't be locked as the bar was part of the boatman's personal equipment, so it was not unusual to discover people sleeping rough aboard these boats. I was told of an incident in pre-war days when some boatmen, arriving to collect a boat from a wharf in Aston Locks, found the cabin full of dossers. They pulled the boat, stern first into an empty lock and drew the centre paddle, thus drenching the cabin and causing a hasty exodus.

Inside the cabin were two built-in benches – one along the right hand side and one placed crossways – and a few hooks for drying wet clothes. All the foregoing tackle belonged to the firm. The boatman's personal equipment included shovels, of which three sizes were commonly carried. The largest was the No.12, used for loading boats where the coal was being shovelled downhill. you could choose between the No.10 and No.8 size for unloading uphill depending on how strong you were and how long and high the throw was. Drinking water was usually carried in a stoneware jar. There was also a bucket for pulling water out of the cut for washing etcetera, a rag mop and a handbrush for sweeping the cabin. Other tackle included a box containing a frying pan, saucepan, plates, knives and forks: many of the older boat people used only a knife for eating.

Lastly, each boatman would have a bundle of old 'jackets', their name for overcoats, which not only enabled them to have a change in rainy weather – clothes soon dried in these small, well heated cabins – but were also spread out on the benches at night to serve as bedding. When you spent the night on a Joey boat you slept with your clothes on. As can be seen, there was no small amount of tack to be changed over at the end of each trip.

Just as Joey boating was very different from cabin boating, so the men tended to use a different language from their long distance counterparts. To them a trip was a 'voyage', the 'Bottom Road' was the 'Old Cut', and anything convenient was 'gain'. To complete a voyage in one day (to do which one had to 'persevere') was to 'run it out'. A rubbish boat which was likely to provide a useful haul of scraps of brass and copper was a 'tat boat', and it was a boatman's dearest wish 'to have the tat boat for Christmas'.

In the winter of 1954, the older boatmen working for Elements on the Old Cut were Tommy Platt, an old steam-boat man who worked with his son also named Tommy, Dicky Parkes, who had also worked on F.M.C.'s steam fly-boats, and Albert Barlow who hailed from Brentford where he had worked on the horse-drawn barges which used the southern end of the Grand Union. Assisting them were various youths, including Albert Rookes and Michael Cusack and a boy we always called 'Sunlight Harold' (a reference to a popular brand of soap) who earned his nickname by always having a dirty face. He was a good natured youth who, despite being kicked by a horse on his first day at work, was very keen on the job.

One or two other lads of school age used to hang around on evenings and weekends, sometimes 'playing the wag', when they should have been at school, so as to have a trip to Pooley or Cannock. They could earn themselves a few bob for doing odd jobs like throwing the water out of a boat's hold with a shovel, or helping to load at Saltley Sidings. I used to get some of them to give the engine hole a good clean on Sunday mornings. Meanwhile they were familiarising themselves with boating techniques, so that if they came to work on The Cut after school they would already have acquired considerable expertise. Prominent among these boys was Michael Cusack's young brother, Brian, who was a keen boxer and only too willing to wind paddles and shovel coal to improve his stamina.

I became particularly friendly with Dicky Parkes, spending many an hour drinking with him in "The Dog" or 'The Muckman'. Dicky, who had been born on a Josher at Nottingham, claimed to be seventy, though Rose and Joe Skinner told me this was an exaggeration. He lived at Ladywood, not far from Gas Street Basin, and it was his habit to walk the four miles to Salford Bridge by six in the morning. Dicky had a great fund of boating stories to tell.He had worked on the Fellows, Morton & Clayton steam fly boats running non-stop between London and Birmingham. As the youngest member of the crew it had been his task, on arrival at London, to scrub out the cabin, including taking up the false floors and scouring the main bottom of the boat until it was white, while the rest of the crew enjoyed – rather briefly, for there was a quick turnround – the fleshpots of the City Road.

As a young man he had taken charge, finding his own horse and mate, of a boat belonging to the paper manufacturers Smith, Stone & Knight, trading between their works at Saltley and Rochdale. This long journey, of 115 miles over the waters of seven different canals, involved legging through the one and a quarter mile bore of the original Harecastle Tunnel. In places the roof would skim the tops of the bales and Dicky recounted how it was necessary to leave a hollow in the bales when loading into which the legger, who lay on top of the cargo, could retreat when the roof came too close. On his first journey he had tied up for the night at Marple, among a group of boats engaged in the limestone trade from Bugsworth, and had been astonished to encounter a distant relation.

Dicky would wistfully recall his encounters with the Lancashire mill girls. "You only had to catch their eye as you walked through the factory," he would tell me, hinting at the sexual conquests of his heyday. He was wont to sum up a lifetime's experience of women in the telling phrase: "They all do it – the only ones that don't are them that hasn't got one!" He was a tough old character. Displaying a set of molars with rather more gaps than teeth, he told me proudly that he had never been to a dentist, but had extracted each aching tooth himself. His fund of stories was as endless as his capacity for beer, for although he drank copious amounts, favouring a mixture of Old and Mild, he never appeared the worse for it. The Old ale, incidentally, was brewed by Atkinsons, and was a most delightful, creamy drink, far superior to the products of the other local breweries. Connossieurs can only regret its demise when Atkinsons were taken over by another brewery.

Having listened to Dicky's stories of the old days when boatmen would live as they could on fish caught in the canal, poached pheasants and rabbits, stolen potatoes (it used to be said that canalside farmers recognised that the row nearest the cut was planted especially for the boatmen) and items filched from cargoes of foodstuffs, I was not surprised one night when we were tied up at "The Dog", to see him fish a dead bird out of the cut, pluck it, put it in the saucepan and consume it with relish when he came back from the pub.

Joey boatmen ate vast quantities of meat (rationing had just ended). It seemed to me that every time an opportunity occurred, on would go the frying pan with its sizzling contents of sausage, bacon or steak topped with a couple of eggs. The relatively big ashpans of the open boat stoves were ideal for baking potatoes, talking of which, I was told a story of when the night soil boats used to unload on to the canalside fields in Curdworth Locks. One day the man employed to empty the boat saw the boatman eating a baked potato. "Let's have one of those," he asked, and stood there munching this baked potato without washing his hands and standing ankle deep in the malodorous cargo.

The cut was so shallow at "The Dog" that loaded boats lay a good way from the shore and you could only get on or off by means of gang plank. One evening, having just made a joking remark to the landlady about the weakness of the beer, I came out of the pub and slipped off the plank into the cut!

The ability to live off the land was vital for old boatmen. Dicky recalled lying at Nottingham for six weeks without a cargo in the days of 'no work – no pay', but remembered that somehow his mother had managed to continue to feed the family. Dicky was now a widower and was fond of going to spend the weekends with one or other of his grown up family. Otherwise his favourite relaxation was to take a ride somewhere on the top deck of a bus. I visited his home in Ladywood, in what was generally thought of as a slum area, but it was spotlessly clean, as was the 'court' in which it was situated. Mind you, some parts of the slums, and there were some bad ones in Aston, were far from salubrious. All the old courts and back-to-backs were soon to be swept away in the post-war slum clearance programme which was to replace many of them with the urine-scented, mugger-haunted tower blocks of the sixties.

Social life at Salford Bridge revolved around 'The Muckman', as the "Erdington Arms" pub was always known, and I soon became accepted as one of the regulars. Birmingham licencing laws were strict. Closing time, or 'putting the towel on', had to be rigidly observed and singing was only allowed in specially licensed rooms. No singing was allowed in 'The Muckman', but there were other pubs which had what were known as assembly rooms and there were two in particular we used to patronise. One in Slade Road, the other being the "Swan Pool" in Lichfield Road. The customary procedure was for those members of the company who fancied themselves as singers to have a go on the microphone. To one or other of these places we would repair on a Saturday night, dodging the girls who hung about outside ready to drink your gin and tonic all evening and then disappear five minutes before closing time.

Albert Barlow particularly fancied himself as a singer and knew a lugubrious ditty which contained such joyous stanzas as:

> *"In her room they found her hanging*
> *With the rope around her neck*
> *By her side they found a letter*
> *This is what the letter said*
>
> *Take this ring from off my finger*
> *Take this necklace from my neck*
> *Give them to my faithless lover*
> *Who has brought me to my end"*

This always went down well with the audience, especially after they had had a few beers. These sing-songs were rather staid occasions with none of the bawdy versions of popular songs that younger lads would treat us to in canalside pubs like the one at Handsacre on the North Stafford. Another of Albert's party pieces was to get his horse to put its head through the door of the bar, which never failed to delight the customers.

I didn't dance, so rarely went to dance halls, but one day when some of us younger boatmen were having the usual boasting session on the wharf, we were joined by a boy we knew who cleaned engines at Saltley locomotive sheds. He claimed to know a dance hall which was patronised by a girl called 'Filthy Alice' who would be smuggled into the gents where she would take on all comers. We decided to go that Saturday. The dance hall was in Erdington, and there were the usual mixture of Teddy Boys (and their female counterparts known in those parts as Teddy Wenches) and more conservatively dressed youths and girls, all of them in their best clothes. The band played a mixture of rock & roll and popular ballads and us non-dancers were quite happy to sit at a table with our beer and enjoy the music and movement. After about an hour our guide nudged us and whispered: "There she is!"

'Filthy Alice' hardly looked a model of depravity. She was a short, plump rather pleasant looking girl of modest demeanour. Nevertheless, as the evening wore on, she was indeed smuggled into the gents by a couple of boys, though the long, eager queue that we expected didn't materialise. We had done a lot of boasting about what we were going to do with 'Filthy Alice', but now we had the chance everyone got cold feet and many were the lame excuses that were trotted out for sitting tight. A boy known as 'Bonzo', however, who we suspected of never having had a girl, was primed with unaccustomed quantities of beer and allowed himself to be persuaded to take his chance. He returned ten minutes later, his unusually clean face a mixture of embarassment and triumph. Shortly after a beaming Alice emerged from her lair, the last waltz signified the end of the evening, and we all piled out to catch the bus back to Salford Bridge. No one wanted to go home so we all went aboard the *New Hope* for a brew of tea and a fry up, during the consumption of which we began to tease 'Bonzo' as to the possible, indeed we soon persuaded him, almost inevitable consequences of his rash escapade.

All possibilities of further amusement having been extracted from the situation, everyone decided to spend the night aboard, no one being the slightest bit bothered about the discomfort of five people crammed into such a small place. 'Bonzo' was threatened with banishment to the back-end coal bunker but was eventually allowed to sleep on the floor. However, the back end did end up with an occupant in the shape of another reveller who turned up and who we were quite unable to squeeze into the cabin. He had to sleep on the coal of course, but at least had the canvas covered back-end beams to protect him from the weather.

I was soon recognised as a regular habitue of 'The Muckman', becoming pally with a young lady of fairground family origins. Her mother kept a nearby boarding house and her stepfather was the local bookies runner. Older readers will recall that there were no betting shops in those days and this illegal method was the only way, off the course, that working people could have a flutter on a horse. On our first date I was disconcerted to find that Josie drank beer by the pint in an age when women always drank halves. Josie had been a tram conductress and, of course, I was avid for details of her experiences. One day she had become so scared by the speed with which a tram was descending Gravelly Hill, she had pulled the trolley pole off the wire, thinking that it would bring the car to a halt. Of course it had no such effect, but despite my patient explanations she could never understand why.

Salford Bridge in those days was like an urban village and I soon got to know lots of people living there. Opposite the wharf was a small corner shop and grocery, and because the owner knew I was 'off the boats', and also because it was my habit to buy large amounts of groceries at a time, I was invited to knock him up if I ever needed food out of normal shopping hours. It was always pleasant to shop at these places where you often got a bar of chocolate thrown in if you had a large order, and regulars were given a glass of sherry at Christmas. Leamington Road also boasted one of those peculiar Brummie institutions, a 'coffee shop'. The name is misleading, as the customers invariably drank tea. There were many such establishments providing a customary fare of bacon, sausage or egg sandwiches. Often, as in this case, their premises had been converted from the front room of a house.

On the main road by the canal bridge were all the usual shops, one of the most important being an ironmongers where I bought paraffin, lamp glasses, Brasso and black-lead. Across the road on the Birmingham side of the bridge was a laundry and, of great importance to the local boatmen, a scrapyard where their carefully hoarded bits of scrap brass and copper could be sold. Boatmen always had their eye open for a bit of 'tat' and would carefully sift through cargoes of rubbish boats for it. I often acquired lengths of copper wire in the process of raking out the blades. but the best source of scrap was the famous 'Tat Boat' which loaded at the Electricity Board's maintenance works at Chester Street in the Aston 'Eleven'. Large amounts of copper wire and brass fittings were thrown, with scant regard for economy, into this boat, the movement of which was the jealously guarded preserve of the New Cut boatmen at Salford Bridge. Needless to say it was given a thorough going over on its journey to Moxley tip.

I had not long been working for Elements when I was introduced to Saltley Sidings, being sent there to load a consignment of coal for the firm of Constructors Limited at Holly Lane Bridge in the 'Four Mile'. The coal had come by rail from a colliery in the Leicestershire coalfield. Taking the turn at Salford Junction on to the Warwick & Birmingham Junction Canal, I came almost immediately to a stop lock known as Saltley Shallow Lock, adjacent to a boatyard belonging to the nearby Nechells Power Station. The power station had a large basin which could be entered from either end and where several grabs were busy on an assembly of coal boats. Nechells was at that time exclusively supplied from Grove (Brownhills) Colliery on the Cannock Extension Canal. The boats belonged to the Electricity Board themselves, whilst towage was provided by the firm of Leonard Leigh, their tug pulling four boats at a time. Additional boats were worked by Element's men and horses under contract to Leighs. Beyond the power station the cut went under Aston Church Road, Saltley Sidings lying on the outside of the canal between the bridge and the entrance to a small reservoir known as 'the lagoon'. It was possible to wind in its entrance.

The wharf was about 250 yards long and flanked by a siding on to which were placed the wagons for transhipment. It served a large number of local firms including G.E.C., Tubes Ltd. (below Aston Locks) and others as far away as Cannings jam factory on the Icknield Port Road Wharf loop line, to reach which meant negotiating the 24 locks of The Eleven and The Thirteen. Saltley Sidings dealt with coal from collieries not served directly by canal, and to works not connected with the railway. Coal was also transferred via the Sidings to supplement supplies where, as for instance on the Old Cut, there was a shortage of boatmen preventing the carriage of a firms entire supply of coal by water. In a severe freeze up the longer distance boats would stop and all work would be concentrated on Saltley Sidings until the canal had thawed again.

Saltley Sidings was a supreme example of rail-canal co-operation. Everyone was happy with it, British Railways, the boatage contractors, and especially George Element who positively chortled at the thought that the casual labour largely used did not incur such complications as insurance stamps and holiday pay. Loading boats at Saltley and man-handling them to nearer works was a popular casual occupation for people who did not want to be tied down to a regular job. At a time when a labourer's daily wage was only about 25/- a day, they could earn more than that loading just one boat at 1/- per ton, a task which might only take a couple of hours. Regular boatmen were pleased that when the cut became iced up, they didn't have to struggle through the ice to Cannock or Pooley, but could go and load round at the Sidings, it being much easier to keep the ice broken on the relatively short distances between there and the local works.

This was my first visit to the Sidings and, having winded by the entrance to the lagoon, I sought around for advice, happily finding Bill Stevens

Junior and his mate Fred Hadley hard at work loading a boat for the Premier Electric factory at the top of Saltley Locks. The first job was to locate the wagons with your coal in, readily ascertained from labels attached to the solebar of each wagon, and position the boat alongside the relevant length of wharf, secured by the 'log' or half hundredweight weight, the rope of which was tied to the shore and the weight hung over the boat's side to enable it to be moved about while loading. Lying about the Sidings were a number of corrugated-iron sheets known as 'tins', and we rigged up one of these below the wagon door, supporting the other end with a wooden prop. Bill explained that when the door catches were knocked up, the door would drop and there would be a sizeable run of coal until it reached its angle of repose inside the wagon. At this stage it was a good idea to enlist some help so as to direct the run into the boat's hold and stop as much as possible from falling on the wharf. This was done by holding up a shovel on each side of the door to direct the flow. The men working on the wharf were always ready to help one another with this job and it only took a few minutes. Once the run had finished you climbed into the wagon and began to scoop the coal out onto the tin using a No.12 shovel. The old type of wooden bodied wagon was still common at Saltley, and when you got down to shovelling on the floor, you had to be careful that the shovel didn't catch in a splinter and give your arm a nasty jar. The more modern 16 ton steel wagons were much more 'gain'. Of course, you had to climb in and out of the wagon several times as you emptied it, so as to move the boat along and get the required trim.

It was still early when I had finished loading, so I decided to go straight on to Constructors and start unloading . First, however, I was asked to tow two Joey boats as far as Salford Junction, from where they would be bow-hauled to the G.E.C. Constructors' factory which was quite typical of an old fashioned canalside works. The coal was shovelled direct, using a No.8 shovel, into the stoke-hold through several windows. As usual there was not enough space to unload, so it was necessary to keep climbing out of the boat to trim the coal back. To make it worse the windows were rather higher than usual, and lack of dredging meant that the boat didn't lie right against the side. I got about a third of the coal out that afternoon and finished the following day, proceeding down to Pooley to load for the G.E.C. The rate from Saltley to Constructors, including loading and emptying, was 5/6d per ton.

CHAPTER EIGHT

BACKWOODS BCN

·

A
lthough *New Hope*'s Ruston engine was very reliable, I had been having some trouble with the water-cooling system, which wasn't surpris-
ing considering the shallow state of the Old Cut. This was causing so much
difficulty that I decided to let Ted Jones overhaul it completely while I
went to Pooley with a horse and Joey boat.

It was January and the canal had frozen overnight, so we had to wait for
the ice-breaker before being able to get away at 9 a.m. with an empty boat
for Pooley where we changed into the already loaded *Lily*. As we had started so late we only got back as far as "The Park" at Kettlebrook, from where
my mate, 'Cakey Bill', went home on the bus; telling me to start without
him if he was late in the morning. It may come as a surprise to many people to discover that horse-boats were sometimes worked single-handed.
This was usually only done for short periods, but I knew one boatman who
had worked from Griff Colliery to Oxford with a horse-boat by himself. He
came back two-handed though, having met a young lady, who later
became his wife, in "The Brittania" at Thrupp.

We had a supply of 'bankers', pieces of coal with the grain running
across which could be used to keep a fire alight all night, so the stove was
still alight in the morning, giving me the unusual luxury of waking up to a
warm cabin. Putting the kettle on, I went to the stable and gave the horse
a feed before going back and having a cup of tea and a piece of bread and
butter. Then I pushed the fore-end over, and threw the end of the line
across to the other shore, before going to gear up the horse and lead him
over the bridge to the towpath where I pegged him to. Back on the boat, I
untied the stern, put the tiller in, shouted "Gee-up!" and was off, feeling
quite excited as I had never worked a horse-boat single-handed before.
The tow-line tightened and the 'elum' gripped the water as we gathered
way. All was going well until I approached a maintenance boat, unattended and tied up on the towpath side. Leaving the tiller, I went forward,

scrambling over the piles of coal, and cast off the tow-line from the mast, letting the horse drag it along the towpath until he was clear of the other boat. As *Lily* drifted past the obstruction, I dexterously caught hold of the tow-line again with the long shaft and replaced the eye on the mast.

I had hoped 'Cakey' would put in an appearance before I got to Fazeley Junction, but no one was in sight as I approached it. As soon as the horse had gone under the turnover bridge I stopped him, then went forward and got off the boat as her fore-end entered the bridge-hole, dropping the line around the fore stud as I did so. Coiling up the line, I carried it over the bridge and, as soon as the stern had cleared the bridge, I took a turn on the stump, placed there for the purpose, and started to check her round the right angle turn towards Birmingham. Being loaded, she carried enough way to keep her moving. As soon as she was well into the turn, I shortened up the line and pegged the horse to, pulling the boat right round into the next bridge-hole. After letting out the line to its full length, I stepped aboard, being joined at the same moment by 'Cakey' who had just got off the bus which crossed the cut at Fazeley. As soon as he was aboard we got the pan on for a substantial fry-up.

I was greatly enjoying this trip. As there were two of us, one could go ahead and get the locks ready, we had no trouble getting stuck on the bottom and above all there was no propellor to become fouled with rubbish. The Pooley – Birmingham Joey boats loaded 23 tons (about 5 tons less than was normal on other parts of the B.C.N) and readers may well ask how it is that they could have a trouble-free journey with this weight while a motor-boat had difficulty with 17 tons. Compared to a cabin-boat, a Joey boat is of very light construction, has no heavy false floors (the bottom being sheared) and doesn't carry the same amount of equipment. For instance, there are no top planks, cratch or stands. This meant that for the same tonnage a Joey boat draws less water than a cabin-boat and it must be remembered that a motor-boat's propellor is sucking water from the side and underneath the boat and, in a restricted channel this will tend to draw the boat towards the bottom of the cut. If a horse-boat does get 'fast' then towage from the bank exerts a greater torque than a propellor and this effort can easily be doubled by rigging up the block which all horse-boats carry.

This was the first time I had steered a Joey boat and, while it was easy enough when loaded, the shallow draught when empty together with a smaller 'elum than a cabin-boat, meant that extra skill was needed to put her in the locks straight and avoid a crosswind which could easily break a plank.

Broken ice tinkling around our bows, we plodded steadily towards Birmingham, not needing to get off to drive the horse until we reached Curdworth Bottom Lock. I had driven the horse down the locks on the way out to Pooley, so now it was my turn to steer going up them. We climbed the eleven Curdworth locks followed by the three at Minworth with 'Cakey' drawing a top paddle, to bring the boat to a stand in the chamber, while I got off and shut the massive single-leaf bottom gate. As the boat rose in the lock I would grab the free end of the block rope and put its eye on the little iron peg set in the extreme end of the lock copings, so that the horse could, in the manner already described accelerate us quickly out of the lock. Incidentally, the curious will look in vain for one of these iron pegs, with which every narrow lock was once provided at top and bottom; British Waterways appear to have removed every single one.

On arrival at the G.E.C. we changed our tools over into an empty boat, and when we had dropped back down stern first to Salford Bridge, that was the end of our day's work. I had enjoyed the trip so much that I decided to do one the next day, this time accompanied by Albert Rooke whose mate was off sick. We brought back the *Nancy*, stopping overnight at "The Dog".

When we got back to Salford Bridge the following morning, I took the advantage of the ice free conditions to start up *New Hope* and go down as far as "The Dog", but it started to freeze again and after two more days I was experiencing heavy ice. On the third, tied up at 'The Bakehouse' going down empty, I had to wait for the icebreaker, afterwards taking eight hours, twenty minutes from 'The Bakehouse' to Pooley as against the usual four and a half hours. After loading the next day I again had to wait for the ice boat, not being able to get away until one in the afternoon.

In the chamber of Curdworth Bottom Lock I picked up a bladeful of rubbish which no efforts could remove so I was forced to tie up there for the night. After much struggling I eventually managed to remove a complete set of bedsprings, old sacks and assorted bits of rope and wire before being able to make a late start, again in thick ice which meant that I only got up as far as 'The Bakehouse'. Once again I had to wait for the ice boat and the delay made me too late to empty at Witton that day. My log records "heavy ice and snow."

I had been getting more and more worried about the undue wear and tear on *New Hope* caused by shocking state of the Old Cut. The episode at Curdworth Bottom Lock, which was only one of many, was the last straw, so I told George Element that I would have to finish working on this job. I had it in mind either to work in the North-west or to go back to the

Coventry Light job, which, if poorly paid, incurred little in the way of wear and tear. His reply was to raise the rate to 6/- per ton and suggest I put a lighter load on (I had been averaging about 18 tons per load). So I was persuaded to stop on.

The cut was now thoroughly iced up, so next day I left the boat to be emptied and went out on the ice-breaker. The Salford Bridge ice-boat was one of the old horse-drawn type. When its services were needed Elements provided the horses and two men to each horse. We went up the New Thirteen, the first time I had been up them, with three horses, accompanied by a gang of 'Company's Men' (British Waterways maintenance workers) whose job it was to clear the huge lumps of broken ice from the lock chambers and to rock the boat, which had a bar running fore and aft for them to cling to, so as to break up the ice.

Ice breaking is a dramatic sight. The boat rolls almost gunwhales under as the horses drag it forward at a run, ice cracking and splintering around its bows. Sometimes it was necessary to stop and take a second run when we encountered a particularly thick patch. There were half a dozen loaded boats waiting to be released from the ice at the top of the 'New 'Uns', but before any more work was done we had to assuage the ravenous appetites created by the vigorous exercise and the cold weather. By the top lock was a 'coffee house' much frequented by boatmen, and we were soon ensconsed in its cosy, steamy warmth, wolfing down bacon sandwiches washed down with mugs of tea. The inner man refreshed and fortified, we emerged to the outside world of ice and snow, our breath condensing in the cold air. We had orders to go as far as the bottom of the 'Ganzy' where the Nechells tug and four boats were awaiting release, and here we winded and set off back to Salford Bridge with the tug following in our wake. The ice boat only needed one horse to take it back down the locks, the other two horses and sets of men each bringing down one of the loaded boats which had been released at the top lock.

Ice had now closed the routes from Salford Bridge to the collieries, so my next job was to take *New Hope* to Saltley Sidings and load her for Wilmot Breeden's works at Tyseley. There were two wagons with a total of 21 tons. This was the first time I had been up Saltley locks. There was plenty of water, and the locks were quite convenient to work, but they undoubtedly the dirtiest I had ever encountered. A film of greasy scum covered the water, lock sides and gates, making the footboards so slippery that great care had to be taken. Of course it all attached itself to your boots and soon the boat was plastered with it.

Above Saltley Locks, there is a level pound of about half a mile before a sharp left turn on to the Warwick & Birmingham section of the Grand Union Canal confronts you with Camp Hill Bottom Lock. Also very dirty, though not quite as bad as Saltley, the six Camp Hill locks lifted you up through darksome surroundings, under bridges clamourous with the groan of labouring steam locomotives and the clash of buffers, to Bordesley, where you emerged into the hive of activity that was British Waterways' Sampson Road Depot. Here spotless blue and yellow London boats contrasted with the grubby local traffic besmirched by its long drag through the 'District'. From here, half an hour of gloriously deep water brings you to Tyseley. This trip from Salford Bridge to Tyseley would normally take two and a half hours, but on this occasion, the ice was so bad that it was five hours before I got tied up.

Wilmot Breeden's factory was on the towpath side nearly opposite British Waterways' Tyseley Wharf. Boats were unloaded by the firm's employees using a shovel and barrow direct into the boiler room, an uncomfortable process, as they often preferred to unload by night and would drag the operation out for as long as twelve hours, always managing, for some unknown reason, to keep the boat tipped over at an angle for most of the time. The fairly lengthy delay gave me a chance to explore Tyseley, a job soon accomplished as it is one of Birmingham's duller and more unlovely suburbs. Trying to clean up the outside of the boat was hopeless, and to make matters worse, an extractor fan in the factory wall blew a chemical substance on to the paintwork, which did it no good at all. However, a trip to Tyseley was advantageous as I could refuel at the British Waterways' wharf. There had been no refuelling facilities on the Birmingham & Fazeley Canal and the task of filling the tanks from 40 gallon drums was awkward and tedious.

It was necessary to proceed backwards in reverse for about a quarter of a mile before I could wind and start back to Salford Bridge. Ice was still causing difficulties on the return trip (the broken lumps get behind the lock gates and have to be removed in order to move them) but a thaw was setting in and I was able to make a trip to Pooley, followed by another from Saltley to Tyseley. The rate for this job was 3/9d per ton, which included loading the boat at Saltley, and I loaded 22 tons. On the way down I picked up one wagon load (10 ½ tons) of DS nuts for Constructors, to be delivered on my way down to Pooley.

Because of the wear and tear I was incurring on the Old Cut, I decided to reduce the amount of work I was doing on the G.E.C. as much as possible and, in pursuit of this aim, I not only persuaded George Element to give me a few Tyseley orders but did a bit of Joey boating as well. Freddie

Morton, who had recently left British Waterways to join Elements, was temporarily without a mate, so I did a round trip to Walsall Wood with him. We picked up a rubbish boat at Saltley and took it to the tip at Moxley. This tip belonged to Ernie Thomas, and rubbish boats from all over the B.C.N. went there. On arrival the boats were shafted into the basin, unloaded by grab and the rubbish tipped into an old sand quarry. Of course we didn't wait to unload, but changed boats and set off with an empty one to Walsall Wood. This meant going up Walsall Locks and round the Wyrley & Essington Canal, turning off on to the Daw End Branch at Catshill Junction to reach Walsall Wood Colliery.

Five miles beyond Birchills Junction, where the Walsall Canal joins the Wyrley & Essington, lies Pelsall, junction with the Cannock Extension Canal. The two canals joined amid an expanse of heathland, grazed by the occasional group of gypsy ponies, stretching away into the misty distance towards Cannock Chase. Romantic, mysterious even, the vista was broken only by the indistinct buildings of the Grove Colliery basin on the Cannock Extension Canal. Along both margins of the Wyrley & Essington lay the remains of early shallow coal workings, now just humps and hollows of black spoil, long covered in vegetation. There was a pub, a huddle of cottages, and the toll collector's house at the stop place on the Extension. A couple of abandoned and half submerged boats completed the scene. As we glided across the heath, I was struck with a strong sense of *deja vu*. Its mysterious atmosphere, the lonely moor stretching away into the far distance broken only by the time-worn buildings at Grove struck some forgotten chord in my subconscious. Had I been here before?

At Walsall Wood Colliery we put the horse in the stable on the towpath side and shafted our boat into the basin which lay in the shadow of the screens and winding gear. On the right hand side was a railway siding and two moveable chutes. A wagon stood in position at each of these. Size twelve shovels at the ready, we each clambered into a wagon and shovelled out the remaining coal, about five tons in all. Then we had to heave up the heavy wagon doors and secure them before man-handling the wagons off the siding. The wagons used here were of the steel, 16 ton type. A pinchbar, a long crowbar with its end flattened and bent at an angle to slip between the rail and the wagon wheels, was inserted. Inch by painful inch the first wagon began to move up the slight gradient to the holding siding. This procedure was repeated with the second wagon, then we changed the points and started to bar the loaded wagons, one by one, into place. Once they were moving it was possible to push them until they achieved sufficient momentum on the slight gradient to run themselves. Then we had to think about applying the brakes. In theory the chutes were moveable, but their wheels were buried deep in coal and it was necessary to place the loaded wagons accurately so that their doors would drop between the cheeks of the chutes. When we knocked up the catches, the heavy doors fell with a clang, but the expected 'run' of coal, which I had expected would do a lot of our work for us, didn't materialise. The coal was fine slack, so wet from the washery that not a spoonful fell from the wagon of its own accord. Standing on the sides of the chutes we had to slice into it with our shovels, awkward work until we had made enough room to get inside the wagon. After we had finished putting in our load of about 27 tons, Fred, who lived in Wolverhampton, went home for the night, which I spent aboard our boat in the basin. It was a Leonard Leigh boat, its cabin very cramped compared with the spacious Element cabins.

The morning dawned bright and windless. I was up and had a kettle boiling and the horse fed by the time Fred arrived, and we set off round the long pound to the top of the 'Mosses'. Fred stayed on the towpath with the horse while we negotiated the low railway bridge and the awkward turns before reaching "The Traveller", beyond which the horse was left to its own devices while we devoted ourselves to a good fry-up. Traffic was light, we met only the Nechells power station tug with its empty train, and two Cannock bound boats belonging to R.B. Tudor of West Bromwich, but these had made all the Rushall locks ready and we dropped down them in short order. I have already described the difficulties of negotiating the turn from the Rushall Canal onto the Tame Valley in the direction of Wednesbury, and the turn in the other direction towards Perry Barr was equally awkward. Like many other canal junctions, only the bare minimum of clearance was allowed, and the time taken to get round must have caused some delay in the days of heavy traffic.

Newtown Junction to Perry Barr top lock ('Top of the New 'Uns') was a pleasant stretch, 'valley' and 'rocking' alternating. We always kept a sharp lookout going through Tower Hill cutting where one of our mates had reported sighting two naked young ladies, though we were inclined to think that this was a figment of his overheated imagination. Anyway, it was hardly the weather for sunbathing.

Before long the top lock loomed ahead and I got off to get it ready. The New Thirteen is arranged in a flight of seven separated from the next four by the 'Quarter Mile'. Below these is a pound of about a mile ('The Miler') followed by the last two known as 'Jills', from which we emerged into the crowd of boats always moored at the G.E.C. The locks on the New Thirteen were rather deep but otherwise very easy and quick to work. In many cases the action of drawing the top paddles would automatically close the bottom gates. Gates banging and paddles rattling, we must have made a brave show flying down the locks in the winter sunshine. The long pounds gave us plenty of time to make our boat tidy and Fred had polished brass rings on his chimney and a scrubbed white turk's head on the 'elum'. I hasten to add that it was rare for anyone to ornament a Joey boat in this way. Going down 'The Miler' old hands would be often heard to remark, "That's where all the best boatmen are," their finger pointing towards the vast Witton Cemetery. Another favourite saying was, "It's no good trying to do it all, (referring to work) there'll still be plenty left when we're gone."

Below the locks it was my turn to steer and I thoroughly enjoyed myself as we glided past the assembled boats at Salford Bridge and took the turn on to the Birmingham & Warwick Junction Canal, this one easily negotiated. And so, up Saltley and Camp Hill locks, our nice clean boat getting dirtier and dirtier as we ascended to our mooring for the night at the top of Camp Hill where there was a stable.

After going in to Tyseley, changing boats and returning to Salford Bridge, we were surprised to get orders for Pooley, because Old Cut and New Cut men usually stuck to their respective routes. As we had brought an empty Leonard Leigh boat from Tyseley, we had to change again into the *Samuel Raymond* belonging to Element's, setting off down the Old Cut straight away to tie up for the night at "The Anchor" at Glascote. We had to wait for the boat to be loaded so it was quite late when we got back to Salford Bridge. These four days of Joey boating had earned me £6.17s.6d. There followed a trip to Pooley with *New Hope*, on completion of which I had orders to take her to load at Walsall Wood.

This was the first time I had been up the 'New 'Uns' single-handed. Not only are the locks very deep but it is not possible to step ashore at the tail. Instead there is an iron ladder in the wall below the bottom gates. Normally when working uphill with an empty motor, the boat is allowed to float into the lock out of gear, and is brought to a stand by drawing a bit of top paddle. I soon found out that this didn't work going up the 'New Un's', as the boat would not hold up to the cill but floated out before the bottom gates could be shut. I solved the problem by attaching a line to the back-end rail and used this to check the boat with a turn on the inside ground paddle. Then I closed the bottom gates before drawing the top paddles. The procedure was a bit cumbersome, but I never discovered an alternative. Working uphill locks with an empty motor required two bow fenders (known as bumpers) the lower one, which we used to make out of rolled up coconut matting, being positioned at cill level. This was a popular floor covering at the time and old matting was easily obtained from tips. It used to take one and a half hours to go up New Thirteen single-handed and two hours to descend. Beyond Perry Barr Top Lock the New Cut stretched wide and straight into the distance. There was something invigorating in the air, an atmosphere quite different from the rather depressing Old Cut.

Breakfast had been cooking as I was coming up the locks and, with a good fry-up on the slide in front of me, I shoved in the clutch and set off in high hopes towards Walsall Wood. But there is a fly in every ointment, and in this case it was the loading arrangements at the Wood. On my previous visit there had been two of us to move the wagons about, but it was a different matter single-handed. Pinchbar in hand, I would attack the obstinate vehicles vigorously, often only to have to admit defeat and be obliged to go up to the pit-head and seek assistance. Much depended on the effect of frosty weather on the axle box grease. I was paid the usual shilling per ton for loading, so the amount of time and effort spent on moving wagons was unpaid for.

Not being able to finish loading that afternoon, I completed on the morrow and set sail for Tyseley through half an inch of ice. After the dreadful struggles experienced on the Old Cut it was a delight to have adequate water for a 22 ton load under me. There was no danger of going aground on this route, although some care had to be exercised on the Tame Valley, as any attempt to open the throttle more than a crack would cause the boat to hit the bottom. This applied both to the summit level and the Mile Pound, although soundings taken of the Miler around this time were said to indicate a proper depth, so it must have been full of submerged obstacles which the sounding pole could easily miss. *New Hope's* blades attracted rubbish like a magnet attracts iron filings and it was prudent to use the reverse cautiously, particularly if it was necessary to hold back above the Top of the Mosses and the Top of the New 'Uns. But these were trifles, and you could normally expect a trouble-free voyage to Salford Bridge and beyond to Tyseley. The sub-contract rate from Walsall Wood to Tyseley, including loading, was 8/- per ton.

My log records "heavy ice" on the next Walsall Wood trip, after which I had to go empty to Tipton for weighing. *New Hope* had a Grand Union weighing number (G.U. 12516) and Grand Union tables for calculating the load. But, despite the fact that all the waterways now belonged to British Waterways, the bureaucracy of the National Coal Board would not accept the G.U. figures, and required me to obtain a B.C.N. gauging number if I wanted to load at Walsall Wood where the load was calculated by gauging, rather than by re-weighing the railway wagons, as was the practice in the Warwickshire coalfield.

It snowed heavily all the way from Tyseley, down Camp Hill and up Ashted and the Old Thirteen, and was still snowing when I arrived at Tipton Factory Locks where the weighing station was located. The operation was done under cover, the boat's dimensions being measured, after which successive one ton weights were craned into the hold, the freeboard (or 'dry side') measurement being recorded after each ton. After 26 tons the rest was done by calculation up to 35 tons which *New Hope* was notionally supposed to be able to carry with half an inch of freeboard. For more practical purposes, she drew 2ft 9ins of water with 17 tons and 3ft 3ins with 23 tons. The nominal maximum draught on the B.C.N. was 3ft 6ins (26 tons) and, generally speaking, you could navigate anywhere, except on the Old Cut, with 23 tons. After all the calculations had been done, two cast iron BCN Plates (B.C.N. 2370) were screwed on to the back end and I was presented with a Gauging Table (whose entries were identical with the G.U. one) and a bill for £1.10s.7d.

I stayed at Tipton for the night, going from there to Walsall Wood the next day. It was nice to be back on the Main Line, with its deep water, as far as Horseley Fields Junction, where I turned off on to the Wyrley & Essington Canal. There were a few factories and coal wharves on the first mile of the Wyrley, but before the war its route had been largely rural as far as Bloxwich, where there was a concentration of old industry. The first place of interest was Wednesfield Junction where there was a stop place and the Bentley Canal led off down a flight of locks on the right hand side. Down the locks was the works of the Weldless Steel Tube Co.. This was served by Leonard Leigh coal boats which were usually towed by an old Josher motor, the *Monarch*, belonging to Roland Wood who lived in a canalside house at Short Heath, and who also kept an old Severner as a spare motor. *Monarch* brought the boats from the colliery to Wednesfield Junction from where they were bow-hauled down the locks. Also down the Bentley Cut was the Wolverhampton Metal works from where gunmetal was boated to Weston Point by British Waterways boats. This contract, however, was not regained until 1957, so was not operating at the time of which I am writing.

Rural, in the context of the Black Country, meant pastureland mixed with the remains of old mineral workings. New housing estates were fast encroaching on this part of the cut, with the result that, although there was a fair depth of water, heavily loaded boats used to have to creep along because of the danger of hitting obstacles on the canal bed. Where there were housing estates the canal immediately became used as a rubbish tip. As in the rest of the Black Country, some intriguing place names were to be found round the Wyrley. Devil's Elbow Bridge, Olinthus Bridge and New Invention were a few. New Invention, which was the name of both a pub and a village, referred to a Newcomen steam pumping engine that had been used for pumping water from local mines. The nearest mine to Wolverhampton that was still working was Hilton Main, and I was soon passing its loading basin at Holly Bank. Here boats were loaded for a variety of destinations, including Walsall and Wolverhampton power stations, Stewarts & Lloyds Tubes at Coombeswood near Halesowen and Noah Hingley's wrought iron works at Netherton. Coal was brought down to the basin in railway wagons hauled by a gleaming National coal board steam locomotive. Each wagon held three containers which were lifted out by crane and positioned above the boats to be loaded, the coal being dropped into the boat through doors in the container's bottom. Each box held about two and a half tons, a similar method was used to load boats at the Cannock & Rugeley colliery basin at the extreme end of the 'Edgeford Arm.

After passing Roland Wood's place at Short Heath, houses gave way to relatively open countryside of the typical Black Country sort. Beyond Adam and Eve Bridge there was an attractive coppice of birch trees on the left, whilst on the other side, Bloxwich lay a mile away across a valley littered with allotments, tin roofed shacks and the occasional gypsy encampment, through which trickled the headwaters of the River Tame. The canal followed the valley northwards as far as Sneyd Junction, where the disused Sneyd and Wyrley Bank Canal rose through five locks to run through fields, old coal workings and brickworks to Wyrley Wharf.

There is an acute turn at the Sneyd and the Wyrley & Essington doubles back on itself to head south-east as far as Birchills Junction. By canal it was three miles from Short Heath to Birchills, a distance of only one mile as the crow flies. The canal route from Wolverhampton to the colliery basin at the end of the Anglesey Arm (known to boatmen as 'Cannock') was 18 miles long as against a direct distance of 8 ½ miles, whilst the 13 ½ miles separating Tipton Factory Junction from the end of the Anglesey Arm was no less than 22 ½ miles by the lock free Wyrley route. The latter journey could be done more directly in those days by way of the Tipton Green & Toll End Communication, thus reducing the distance to 17 miles, the shorter route involving 18 locks. At the Sneyd was one of the Birmingham Canal's principal maintenance depots, the other being on the Icknield

Port Road Wharf Loop.

Half a mile beyond Sneyd lay the old industrial area of Bloxwich where a happy juxtaposition of iron ore, coal and limestone had led to the establishment of an extensive iron industry. Some of the works, which, in the fashion of our industrial dawn, boasted names such as Phoenix or Alpha on their tall, belching chimneys, were now given over to the processing of non ferrous metals. Such a works was International Alloys, probably the largest individual customer for canal borne zinc, which entered the country at Liverpool, Manchester, London and, increasingly in the late 1950s, Avonmouth. The eye looked in vain for boats at this waterside works, as all the zinc was unloaded and stored at various wharves in Birmingham, and also on the River Severn at Worcester and Stourport, from where it was delivered by road under the system known as 'controlled delivery', whereby a specified amount was sent to the works each day. In 1956 Diglis Wharf at Worcester alone was sending 80 tons a day to this one customer.

A little further on, where the Bloxwich road crossed the cut, there were two busy boatyards, that of Worsey's on the left before the bridge, and that of Peter Keay's on the right beyond it. The mainstay of these yards was the maintenance of the large fleet belonging to the British Electric Authority used to supply coal to the power stations at Wolverhampton, Walsall and Ocker Hill. Most of these were ordinary Joey boats, but there were also a number of redundant Severn & Canal Carrying Company horse-boats, very suitable for this work as they had a hull shape not very different from a Joey boat and cabins hardly any longer. Former long distance boats with fine lines were useless for this work because the large grabs used by the power stations could not work forward of the mast beam. Ex Josher butties were usually employed as rubbish boats for this reason.

Although Walsall Light was supplied from several collieries, the ex Severners were, for some reason, confined to the Holly Bank to Walsall traffic, never going to 'Cannock' or Hednesford. Nor did they work on the Holly Bank to 'Wolverhampton Light' run. Towage to both these power stations from Holly Bank was done by Leonard Leigh, whilst the run to Walsall from other collieries was contracted to Ernie Thomas whose headquarters were at Walsall Top Lock. Leonard Leigh had purpose built tugs for the trade, whereas Ernie Thomas's were shortened Josher motors fitted with tractor engines burning T.V.O. Ocker Hill Light was also served by Ernie Thomas, but by horse towage from Sandwell Colliery Wharf on the Old Main Line at Smethwick.

The Wyrley & Essington was a heavily used canal, most of the trade being coal conveyed in trains of four or five boats hauled by a tug. Before the introduction of this system in the 1930s, traffic to Tipton and beyond was hauled by horse and travelled via one of the several shorter, but heavily locked, routes. Motor-boats, which carried a fairly light cargo as well as towing, were few and far between because of the delay occasioned to crews while they were unloaded. The Wulfruna Coal Company of Wolverhampton had one, captained by Bill Tolley, and R.B. Tudor of West Bromwich and S.T. Brant of Winson Green also had one apiece. In these cases the boatmen were employed to unload them by hand, so there was no idle time. Elements had a motor which they used in the Oldbury to Tipton phosphorous waste traffic, plus another laid up at their Oldbury dock. Of course, motors could sometimes be seen in the short distance tar trade, still, at this time, mainly the province of Black boats, but not often until the demise of the Port Claytons in 1956 made a number of motors available.

With the tug and train system well established, and the alternative of 'carrying' motors also possible, it will no doubt be asked why horse towage still survived on the B.C.N. Not from sentiment, I can assure you. Take the Sandwell to Ocker Hill Light job, for instance, with its eleven locks in a four mile trip. The only possible way this could have been mechanised would have been by push-towing, where a tug would push a shortened boat, the combined length not exceeding that of a lock. By the time this system had been tried and tested on the B.C.N., the writing was already on the wall for the local coal trade. A similar traffic situation was the movement of rubbish boats from Albion to Moxley.

Although one tug worked through Salford Bridge en route between Brownhills and Nechells Light, none of the other Salford Bridge traffic was suitable for towage, the Old Cut being impractical for trains of boats and the remaining traffic off the New Cut being impossible to organise to suit tug towing because it was not capable of concentration, being drawn from so many different collieries. Some boats were routed up empty via The Ganzy to Walsall Wood, Brownhills and 'Cannock', others returned with rubbish via Moxley. While Walsall Locks, The Ganzy and the New 'Uns were reasonably convenient for the bow-hauling of a train of boats, Saltley and Camp Hill locks were not.

Carrying motors could assist with the traffic (I was doing so myself), but complete mechanisation of say, the Pooley to G.E.C. job would have been impossible, because all those individual motor boats would have delayed each other waiting loading and unloading to an extent which would have reduced the amount of work capable of being done by each man. The Joey boat system of changing from one boat to another meant that boats could be left to be unloaded and loaded at the customer's convenience (it might take a week for a rubbish boat to accumulate a load at some places)' while the men and horses and moveable capital equipment could carry on working. All these objections could have been met by push-towing but, as it was never introduced except in isolated cases, horse haulage remained the only practical method for Element's traffic in the Salford Bridge area. I am writing, of course, of 1954/5. Later, changes in trade and circumstances did permit some limited mechanisation of this traffic, but for the moment the horse reigned supreme.

On the Wyrley & Essington Canal there were short runs to the power stations where each tug did more than one trip per day, jobs such as the Weldless Steel Tube where the tug did just one trip per day and longer trips to Tipton and beyond of longer than a day's duration. Here the usual practice was to work out to the coalfield and back on Monday, Wednesday and Friday, and spend the next day delivering the boats to their destination. for instance, Element's Oldbury tug, the *Princess Anne*, captained by 'Yampy Tom' Evans might, on a Monday, bring in two boats for Chance's glassworks at Smethwick, one for British Industrial Plastics up 'The Crow' (Titford Canal), and one for Bellis & Morcom in Birmingham. To deliver these boats on Tuesday would be only a short day's work.

But the day the tugs went out to the coalfield was long and gruelling. The return voyage between Tipton and 'Cannock' would take at least thirteen hours. On the journey out the empty boats were tied close together, the tug driver isolated on his tug and relieved only for breakfast, while the others took their ease in the cabin of the last boat, someone emerging to straighten it up when necessary. At the colliery the laborious process of changing tools had to take place and the outgoing loaded boats, selected from dozens of others, shunted about to form a train. The voyage back loaded was a different matter, involving at least nine hours at the tiller without a break, unable to stop even if you wanted to as the tug dragged you remorselessly onwards. Of course, you usually had a stove, and could stand on the footboard with the doors closed behind to keep you warm, and you could make tea and warm up some food to be eaten at the helm. Minor calls of nature were easily dealt with simply by urinating over the side, but what, the reader may wonder, would happen if more serious relief were unavoidable? The answer is that the boatman waited for an unfrequented length of canal, free from navigational difficulties as well as houses and passers-by, lowered his trousers and perched on the edge of the hatches with his posterior projecting over the water, one hand clutching the tiller. Needless to say, the continued encroachment of housing estates along the cut was a hindrance to this time-honoured practice. Nelson's seamen managed in much the same way.

Still, it was not all bitter winds and blizzards. There were sunny days and starry nights when the roaring fire easily defeated the first hint of frost. And there was always the chance that a young lady might leap aboard and, having thrown a quantity of coal on to the towpath to be recovered later, keep you company for a mile or so. On the return trip the tug driver might leave you floating about at Pelsall Junction while he went up and collected a boat from Brownhills Colliery. But normally they endeavoured to get a full train from 'Cannock' or off the 'Edgeford Arm on separate days. If this wasn't possible, they would try and make informal arrangements for another tug to bring an odd boat as far as Pelsall where it would be left until its own tug arrived.

The Wyrley had, for the most part, a restricted channel and abounded with awkward bends, blind bridge-holes and overhanging trees. One of the worst places was just beyond Peter Keay's dock, and it was here I chose to meet an Ernie Thomas tug hell bent for Walsall Light with five on. These tugs were usually about forty foot long and ballasted just enough to give fan hold, so they were quite shallow draughted. It would not surprise me to learn that their throttles were fully opened at the colliery and not closed again until they reached their destination or had to stop for gauging. The trains of boats (a Joey boat drew about 2 feet 9 inches of water with 27 tons) were dragged through bridge-holes and stop places without slackening speed, and no concessions were made to boats going the opposite way. It does not take much imagination to understand the difficulties of passing one of these trains of boats with a much less manageable empty motor, with the tug and train drawing all the water out of the cut with their speed and spread out over a total length of about 150 yards.

I had eased right down, as was the custom, but the tug came on at full speed, the steerers pushing frantically on their tillers to get round the bend. I managed to pass the first two boats without mishap, but abreast of the third, my stern caught the bottom of the cut and, out of control, I ended up in the trees. Mop, shaft, watercan and chimney were swept from the cabin top, but the last two items were well secured and hung from their chains. Fishing the mop and cabin shaft out of the water, I managed to get off the bottom and proceeded with no more damage than a bit of scratched paintwork.

This was the last tug of the day and the rest of the afternoon passed uneventfully. Beyond Keays' boatyard the cut wound through Coalpool and Goscote (where boats sometimes loaded copper at Elkington's works

"Summat up mister?"

Breaking the ice, BCN style.

for Brentford or Sherborne Street) followed by Little Bloxwich, where the sharp turn after Teece's Bridge was known to boatmen as 'Benny's'. This was one of the few places on the Wyrley where it was convenient to tie up for the night. More open country followed before the canal crossed Pelsall Common, to wind on through old spoil heaps, clumps of birch and open fields to skirt Brownhills and reach Catshill Junction. Alongside the cut at Brownhills was a row of cottages which rejoiced in the name of Shithouse Row because their outside privies backed on to the canal. Here boatmen would surreptitiously drop sacks of coal into the water for the inhabitants to fish out after dark.

Tied up at Walsall Wood, I reflected on the day's events and resolved to time future excursions on to the busy waters of the Wyrley so as to avoid as far as possible meeting loaded tug trains when I was empty. This was easily done as the tugs adhered to the same routine week after week and the places where you might meet them were easily predictable. Tuesday, Thursday and Saturday were quieter than other days and there was no trade on Sundays. Because everyone started early, traffic was rarely still on the move by late afternoon.

Ice was still causing me problems. There was a prolonged delay in loading at Walsall Wood due to the railway wagons being iced up and, once I got going, *New Hope* was brought to a stand by ice on the far side of Aldridge. Being so exposed, this bit of canal always iced up more readily than some places. I had to await release by the icebreaker at eleven, and I didn't reach Tyseley until ten in the evening, not daring to stop in case I became frozen in again.

Unloading wasn't completed until midnight on the following day, after which I struggled back down to Salford Bridge. The routes to the collieries were now closed by ice and I spent the next fortnight loading boats at Saltley Sidings and moving coal and rubbish boats around the local area. The following list gives an idea of the sort of work we did when the main routes were closed by ice and what we were paid for it.

23/2	rubbish	Saltley to Salford Bridge	5s.0d
24/2	coal	Salford Bridge to Tyseley	£1.5s.0d
25/2	rubbish	Tyseley to Salford Bridge	£1.5s.0d
28/2	loading boat at Saltley (25 tons)		£1.5s.0d
2/3	loading boat at Saltley (27 tons)		£1.7s.0d
3/3	coal	Perry Barr to Salford Bridge	
	rubbish	Salford Bridge to Perry Barr	£1.7s.6d
4/3	emptying rubbish boat at Snow Hill basin		

		and taking empty boat to Windsor St wharf	£1.5s.0d
5/3	coal	Salford Bridge to Tyseley	£1.5s.0d
5/3	rubbish	Tyseley to Saltley	£1.5s.0d
7/3	coal	Saltley to Tyseley	£1.0s.0d
9/3	coal	Saltley to Tyseley (30 tons)	£1.10s.0d
9/3	rubbish	Tyseley to Moxley	£2.0s.0d

By the 9th of March the cut was opening up again, and on that day Freddie Morton and myself loaded a boat at Saltley for Tyseley. Being temporarily short of boats (because of the accumulation of rubbish boats which we had been unable to get away to the tip at Moxley) Elements had to hire one from the Nechells Power Station fleet for this job and, as we had two 16 ton steel wagons containing exactly 30 tons, we decided to cram it all into this boat. When we had finished our little boat didn't have a lot of 'dry side', in fact she looked impressively deep in the water. Despite this we got her up to Tyseley without any trouble, changed into a loaded rubbish boat the same day, and got back to Salford Bridge, going up to Moxley the following day, then round to the Wood. I only worked this boat as far as Salford Bridge as the cut to Pooley was also open again. My complaints about wear and tear caused by the state of the Old Cut had resulted in yet another increase in the rate, this time to 6/6d per ton, but I was determined to get off the job as soon as a good opportunity offered itself. That day, in fact, was not far distant.

CHAPTER NINE

THE
BREWERY RUN

·

Locking up at Glascote one morning, I encountered S.E. Barlow, and in the course of conversation I happened to mention what a pity it was that there was no longer any trade to Oxford. S.E. surprised me by replying that he still had the Morrells Brewery coal contract, but had been sending it by rail because he was short of boatmen. We quickly came to an agreement that I should do the job for him at a rate of 13/6d per ton.

George Element thought I was crazy when I told him I was going to work to Oxford. From a strictly financial point of view it was impossible to equal the earnings attainable in the Birmingham and Black Country district anywhere else on the cut. But money was not the be-all and end-all of my existence. I had chosen boating as a way of life and wanted to enjoy it as much as possible. As I wrote in chapter one, my idea of boating was a smart, spotlessly clean, brightly painted boat, agleam with polished brass and scrubbed woodwork, working briskly over the Midlands waterways system. The desperate struggle to get up the Old Cut, the constant fight against dirt caused, not so much by the filthy state of parts of the Birmingham Canals, as by the almost daily loading and unloading of coal cargoes with all the mess entailed, and the need to strip the boat of all those decorative bits and pieces such as cratch, mast and stands, certainly did not fit in with my vision of what boating life should be like. Nevertheless, the first object of a business is to survive, and the 1954/5 winter working for Elements had left me in a sound financial position.

My estimate was that it would be possible to do the return Griff Colliery to Oxford trip of 81 miles each way in a week, a 23 ton load bringing in £15.10s.6d. A week's work of three trips up the Old Cut grossed about £18.10s with a 17 ton load, total weekly mileage being 102. It was important to take into account the possibility of delays by flood and ice. There were no floods on the B.C.N. and I have already related how it was possible to continue to earn a living in severe ice conditions. The reduced wear and tear of the Oxford route compared with the Old Cut was also a factor. Whatever the arguments, it all boiled down to this: I wanted to extract maximum enjoyment from my boating, and I knew that by living on the boat I could manage comfortably on much less than I expected to earn on the Oxford.

On my last trip to Birmingham I put the cratch, mast and stands back on board, and took a nostalgic look around my favourite haunts, before setting off down the Old Cut to start this new episode in my boating career. To save empty mileage to Griff Colliery Basin I called in at Pooley for a load to Coventry Light, the rate for which had been increased to 4/6d per ton, making my 23 ton load worth £5.3s.6d. There was the usual prolonged wait for unloading at Longford, after which I set off in a state of high excitement to Griff.

Coal from the Griff collieries was loaded at a basin at the end of the Griff Colliery Company's Canal, which left the Coventry Canal 2 ½ miles south of Nuneaton, and ran for six furlongs to Griff Basin to which the coal was brought by internal colliery railway. The entrance was a tiny bridge-hole, embowered in trees, to negotiate which cratch, mast and cabin chimney had to be removed or lowered. The arm was crossed by the A444, beyond which there were chutes for loading stone from the Griff quarries. These were situated on a wide turn in the canal, after which it narrowed and pursued an isolated course through fields on one side and scrub on the other to reach its L-shaped terminus equipped with wooden loading wharves and sidings. I never found out whether the Griff Arm became the property of the National Coal Board or of British Waterways after nationalisation.

Griff Basin never failed to charm me and I loved to spend the night there. There was something peculiarly attractive about this little pocket of old-fashioned industry in its seemingly remote rural setting. An unsurfaced track, running between leafy hedges, connected it with a lane leading to the main Nuneaton to Coventry road three-quarters of a mile distant. In the other direction a set of level crossing gates separated it from the hamlet of Bermuda, a short street of houses so small that its name didn't appear on the one inch Ordnance Survey map. Bermuda was only to be reached from the outside world by means of narrow lanes. It did not boast a pub, but had a Working Mens club of which Joe and Rose Skinner were members.

When I got to Griff mine was the only boat there, and the wagons with my coal had not yet come down from the pit. The first thing to do was to rig up the cratch, which consisted of deckboard, false cratch and cratch boards. The mast box was put back in its proper, upright position, having been taken out of its step and leant against the mast beam at an angle to reduce its height for getting under the bridge at Griff Hollow. The telescopic mast was then raised by about a foot and secured in this position by a pin through a hole in it. The mast plank was placed between cratch and mast and the remainder of the top planks elevated to rest on the mast, tops of the stands, and engine-hole roof. These planks were firmly secured to the stands with bits of line called 'girders' and to the cabin block on the engine-hole cant rail by a length of scrubbed cotton line. Then the cratch was decorated with a length of belting made out of old canvas fire hose. This was tensioned by being attached to the gunwhales by two short bedsprings obtained from an old style metal framed bedstead. In their day, such metal bedsteads had formed the cargo of many a Josher, being loaded at both Fazeley Street and Dudley Port depots. Behind the belting were arranged two lengths of cotton line passing from the gunwhale over the cratch, their ends being arranged in decorative rosettes.

While I was putting the finishing touches to this ensemble, I became aware of rumbling noises in the distance. The level crossing gates were opened and an N.C.B. steam locomotive, highly polished as were most of her kind, trundled a short rake of wagons over, reversing to place them in position on the siding by the loading wharf. The wagons were all of the old fashioned wooden variety, and included three containing my coal, which took the form of moderately sized lumps known as cobbles. The boat loaders had now appeared and, having lit the fire in their hovel and put the kettle on, they started work. The usual procedure was followed, the wagon door dropped and the initial run of coal allowed to fall into the hold, guided by holding a shovel each side, after which the serious business of shovelling began. The men told me that they received sixpence per ton for loading boats, but whether or not this was in addition to a daily flat wage I am unable to say.

I loaded 22 tons 5 cwt of coal, piling it high in the back end and stern middle rooms so as to leave a break behind the mast. A break means that a gap is left in the coal, with it barely covering the floorboards, so that the men emptying the boat can start shovelling on the floors. Unlike the smaller grades of coal, it was difficult to dig into cobbles from the top. Coal was then piled in front of the mast until the correct trim had been achieved. If you needed to get a really big load on, the thing to do was to arrange a plank from one of the beams to the floor, the shovel would then be slid down this under the coal until a bit of floor space was clear.

As soon as loading was completed, I shoved clear of the wharf to allow in a pair of British Waterways boats heading for Croxley Mill at the London end of the Grand Union. The top planks had been up throughout the loading operation, so it only remained to insert the uprights between gunwhale and top plank. These were eight notched lengths of wood which added further support to the top planks, making them firm and rigid enough to walk along. Incidentally, walking – or where necessary, running – along these 18 inch wide planks required some practice to do confidently. Nevertheless, lots of boatmen continued rigging up the top planks when it was really more convenient just to lay them on top of the coal. Between the two extremes there were all sorts of variations. In the Potteries, uphill boats often had all the top planks up, except the one nearest the cabin which would be laid on the beams. This was because it was not necessary to have the side-cloths up along more than three-quarters of the hold to prevent water coming in over the gunwhales when the top paddles in the locks were drawn. Some of the long distance coal boats trading from the Warwickshire coalfield had no side-cloths, their captains considering that they harboured the dirt, which was true, whilst the bigger types of ex Grand Union boats had such deep holds that their freeboard was sufficient for them to leave their side-cloths rolled up on the gunwhales unless the cargo required protection. Others displayed a wide variety of appearence. Some had their stands cut down and a supporting block fitted to the mast, so as to reduce the height of the planks, at any rate behind the mast. Others laid their planks on top of the coal. Some had full side-cloths up, others for the length of about half the hold, others only up as far as the mast.

The process of loading had, as usual, left the boat covered in coal dust, which I attacked vigorously with mop and scrubbing brush. First of all the entire boat was mopped off, the mop being dried by 'trindling', i.e. rolling the mopstick up and down the arm in order to dry off the paintwork afterwards. Then the cratch belting and white cotton ropework were scrubbed, using only water as soap was thought to make them yellow. Cleaning was finished off by scrubbing the ash strips around the counter and fore-end with a metal pan scourer. Soon a spotlessly clean boat emerged from the grime, and I was happy in the knowledge that the cargo would not have to be touched again for another three or four days.

At quarter past two I slid in the clutch and set off on my eighty mile journey to Oxford. Once out of the arm I was back on a main artery of waterway commerce, winding my way towards Sutton's Stop with a pleasingly adequate depth of water under me. At Bedworth Hill, the junction of the Newdigate Arm, a group of boats lay moored outside the pub. Some were waiting to load at Newdigate, others already loaded and spruced up, ready for the long trip to the Home Counties, following the usual custom of not proceeding beyond a nearby convenient tying-up place on the day they loaded, after which it would be hell for leather to their destination. Some boatmen favoured stopping at Bedworth, but the most popular stopping place was Sutton's, and in those days you approached it through lines of moored boats on both sides of the cut.

There is a difficult U turn at Sutton's, difficult, that is, if you were single-handed and without anyone to strap you round with a rope off the fore-end. Without this aid a good deal of 'backing and filling' was needed to get round. I stopped for an hour to oil up and lay in a stock of food. Unlike on some canals, such as the Grand Union and the Cheshire Locks section of the North Stafford, there were few handy shops immediately adjacent to the Oxford Canal. Apart from Newbold, which was only four hours run from Sutton's, and therefore not of much use to southbound boats, the first convenient place to tie up and go shopping was at Banbury, two days journeying distant. The well organised boatman would try and lay in sufficient stocks of food so as to avoid unnecessary tying up to go shopping. Having gone to the trouble of stopping, you were always likely, if it was around teatime, to be tempted to stay where you were, sit down for a meal and go to the pictures instead of pressing on.

Fuelled and victualled, I picked my way gingerly through the double line of moored boats, two abreast on each side of the cut, and proceeded around the sharp and quite difficult turn which separated the junction and the power station. Unloading had ceased for the day and a couple of pairs of Barlow's lay on the towpath side waiting to be dealt with in the morning. More boats lay at Tushes Bridge, a popular alternative tying up place for southbound boats. There used to be a boatyard here on the outside. Beyond Tushes Bridge began the Sowe Common New Cut, running straight as a die for a mile. This part of the 1829-34 improvement of the Oxford Canal cut off two loops, the first to Wyken Old Colliery, of which only one end survived as a reedy bed, rather surprisingly as it was recorded as being disused since as long ago as 1904. The second was the three-quarter mile long Wyken New Colliery loop giving access to the Wyken Colliery Company's canal which had remained open until more recent times.

At the southern end of the New Wyken Loop the original course of the canal is resumed. Oxford lies slightly east of south in relation to Coventry, but for the next mile the cut heads north-east as far as Ansty where, having rounded the notoriously mud encumbered Ansty Turn, upon which many an empty boat had come to grief, it resumes a generally south-easterly course as far as Rugby. It was now getting on towards seven o'clock and, with the stewpot simmering on the range and the prospect of "The Archers" on the radio, I decided to tie up at Stretton Stop, hoping to make Fenny Compton on the morrow. I slept soundly, undisturbed by the constant rattle of night expresses and heavy freights pounding the adjacent West Coast main line.

As it happened, I slept too soundly, for, failing to hear the alarm go off at its accustomed hour of 6 a.m., it was well after seven before I was setting off along Brinklow Straight. The canal was well maintained and loaded boats could keep up a speed of 3 m.p.h. which was good for a narrow canal. Back in January 1950, my very first day's boating had been done on this stretch of cut aboard John Knill's *Columba*. There had been a steam dredger working then, and it was still hard at work five years later. I came across it on the far side of Hall Oaks Wood, surrounded by its attendant mud boats, into which the dredgings were loaded to be taken to a suitable site for discharging. The dredger's name was *Alice*, giving rise to the anguished thought, when you were hard aground on one of the South Eastern Division's less well maintained waterways, of "Alice, where art thou?", the title of a once popular song.

Unfortunately the dredging was not, at that time, simultaneously accompanied by bank protection, and there was a lot of erosion on the North Oxford caused by the constant traffic of motor boats being driven hard along a canal of restricted cross-section. Nowhere was this worse than at Hall Oaks Wood, where the towpath had almost completely disappeared, much to the annoyance of the Skinners who were now the last horse-boaters on the canal. Their repeated and much justified complaints about the state of the towpath received no sympathy from British Waterways' bureaucrats and it remained in a shocking state until horse-drawn traffic had completely disappeared. While working, canal dredgers are held in position by mooring wires attached to both banks, so I had to wait until the wires were dropped on one side for *New Hope* to squeeze past. This was no problem with a loaded boat, but in windy weather empties could be blown on to the mud while they were waiting.

Completed in January 1790, the Oxford Canal originally formed part of a through water route from Lancashire and the West Midlands to London, boats completing their journey to the capital by going down the Thames. Its key position gradually became eroded, firstly by the opening of a shorter route from Birmingham to Braunston via Warwick, and then by the construction of the Grand Junction Canal. Thereafter the Oxford's share of the important London to Birmingham trade was confined to the five miles between Braunston and Napton. Similarly, the Lancashire to London trade also left the Oxford for the Grand Junction at Braunston.

Despite the early loss of its key position as a merchandise carrier, the Oxford remained a busy and profitable canal, paying a dividend right up to nationalisation. A massive trade in coal passed over the northern section en route from the Warwickshire coalfield to the London area, while the city of Oxford, with its well off academics and its draughty halls of learning, was an important market for coal. Even in the country areas the size of some of the wharves, that at Aynho for instance, points to a substantial trade. Apart from domestic consumption, a great deal of agricultural machinery was steam powered, and steam traction engines and steam rollers were once a common sight. The coal trade was supplemented by the carriage of roadstone, quarries of suitable material also being conveniently situated in the Warwickshire Coalfield. By 1955, the main traffic on the Oxford Canal was coal to the Grand Union at Braunston and merchandise on the still busy London to Birmingham route which used the Oxford Canal between Braunston and Napton. South of Napton there had been a drastic decline in trade, and only the occasional coal, tar or timber boat disturbed these otherwise deserted waters.

Passing under the railway near Cathiron, the canal entered a cutting which led to the short Newbold Tunnel, beyond which is Newbold Wharf and village, known to boaters as 'Noble', by far the best tying up place on the northern part of the canal. Soon after, the short arm leading to the Rugby Co-op Wharf goes off under a bridge on the right. Skirting Rugby well to the north of the town, the boatman is soon confronted by the three locks at Hillmorton, the only ones in thirty miles between Hawkesbury and Napton. Beyond Hillmorton lie seven miles of remote canal, alternating between long straights and bits of the original waterway complete with sharp turns, before the triangular junction at Braunston is reached. The right hand curve which I took towards Napton was rather shallow because of the tendency of the heavier traffic on the other two routes to silt it up with the action of their propellors.

The three-quarter mile Braunston Straight marks the last of the Telford improvements, at the end of which the Great Central main line crossed the canal and its original winding course resumes. A Woodford bound coal train rumbled overhead, the driver and fireman of its R.O.D. 2-8-0 waving to me as it passed. I waved back but could not help ruefully reflecting that some of the wagons on that train were quite likely to be destined for Banbury or Oxford in competition with the canal. But such thoughts were soon forgotten as I gave myself up to the enjoyment of what was surely one of the most delightful stretches of canal still in commercial use. Remote and tranquil, it wound its way around bend after bend, under old brick bridges with the patina of almost two centuries of use, only its ample depth of water being a reminder that it was part of an important transport route. Nearly all the traffic was northbound, as most boats arriving at Birmingham from London then proceeded empty to the Warwickshire collieries via the Birmingham & Fazeley Canal. It was all the more pleasurable, therefore, to meet a pair of ex Grand Union boats, high out of the water, with their London bound cargo of rags and empty barrels.

I had not long eased gingerly round the blind turn under the London Midland Leamington to Weedon line (which had a station at Braunston) when the windmill on Napton Hill came into sight, and another three miles brought me to Napton Turn. I was soon to discover that, unless speed was reduced to take the junction, the fore-end of a loaded boat would drop alarmingly when it entered the shallow water caused by the bar thrown up by boats on the more heavily used route. Beyond Napton Turn the cut was much shallower, but it presented no difficulties until I had passed the brickworks, which once owned a boat called the *Windmill*. Beyond the works I came upon the first of the south Oxford's notoriously difficult turns, a right angle inside bend by a farmhouse. Protected by dilapidated wooden piling, it was a real 'cow' to get round with a loaded boat.

Although there may be an adequate depth of water, the passage of boats around such sharp turns tends to form a bank of mud on the inside of the bend, restricting the channel to the extreme outside. If the banks are unprotected, the action of a boat's propellor erodes the outside bank which makes things worse. Unless taken at dead slow speed and with absolutely precise positioning, a loaded boat was likely to end up with her fore-end up the outside bank of the turn, and would then have to do some 'backing and filling', possibly resorting to the use of the long shaft, to get round. Interestingly, these turns presented more difficulty to a single motor than one with a butty hung on behind; they are much easier to get round when towing, partly because the butty pushes water ahead of it, providing a slightly greater depth under the motor, and partly because its weight has a steadying effect, which means that when the motor's helm is put over and the throttle opened to turn, there is less forward movement as the manoeuevre is carried out.

There was another sharp turn immediately below Napton Locks, but this one presented no difficulty, and I was soon at rest in the chamber of the bottom lock. The nine locks at Napton are spaced out over a distance of one and three-quarter miles, there being a flight of six followed by a quarter mile pound before the isolated Greens Lock, the two top locks being nearly a mile further on. The locks were quick and easy to work, being unusual in having cast iron bottom gates.

There were no other boats about, and it was hard to imagine the scene of years ago. Old boatmen had told me of the days when a boat could arrive at the bottom of Napton in the afternoon, and find so many boats in front that it couldn't go up until the following morning. Back in the days of working boats it was never the custom to close lock gates behind you, as is done nowadays, but Napton Top Lock was an exception. The water supplies in the summit level had to be carefully guarded, and we always left the top gates closed at both Napton and Claydon top locks.

Napton flight terminates in the tiny hamlet of Marston Doles, with a disused wharf, which had become part of a farmyard on the outside above the lock. The people who lived here liked to reminisce about the times when they were in the coal trade, pointing out that if they ordered a boatload and a wagon-load of coal at the same time (the nearest station being at Charwelton, nearly five miles distant on the Great Central line) the boat would always arrive first, usually before the invoice!

It was about five o'clock when I came out of the top of Napton Locks and set off round the Eleven Mile Pound. So completely remote that I might have been in another world, the canal wound its lonely way across the Northamptonshire Uplands, attractive rolling countryside of mixed arable and pasture. In eleven miles there was only one canalside habitation, the "George & Dragon" pub at Fenny Compton. For most of the way no building was in sight except for the prominent tower of Napton mill, appearing behind, in front, to one side or to the other as the cut twisted and turned. To be in charge of a smart, heavily laden boat round the 'Leven Mile Pound was, to me, all that could be asked of boating life. I was pleased to find a good depth of water in the summit, but it was well known for its awkward turns, one of which, Cabbage Turn, was infamous all over the canal system for its difficulty. It took four hours and twenty minutes to cover the summit, an average of about two and a half miles an hour, which was good by narrow canal standards, especially when cautious negotiation of the worst bends was allowed for.

I had been contentedly chugging along for nearly an hour, having successfully managed a couple of difficult bends, when I came upon Cabbage Turn. A bed of reeds grew on the towpath side, leaving a narrow lane of water which appeared to terminate in a field. I closed the throttle and pulled out of gear, knowing that I would need to be almost at a standstill when the moment came to push the tiller hard over and apply a burst of power to get round. Almost imperceptibly the heavily laden *New Hope* drifted into the turn, which gradually opened up to reveal that the cut did not end in a field, but continued round a bend so sharp that it almost doubled back on itself. The outside bank was almost within spitting distance of my fore-end when I judged the time was right for action. Slamming in the clutch, I opened the throttle wide and forced the tiller hard over to port, the deflected water shooting out in an impressive spray from under the counter. Having practically lost all way, the *New Hope* started to turn with hardly any forward movement, and in a moment I was round, the channel lying straight and clear in front of me. Throttling back to cruising speed, I lit a celebratory cigarette and relaxed.

Cabbage Turn was not the only bad bend on the summit however. An early dusk was falling as threatening black clouds gathered overhead. It was pitch dark and raining heavily when I came to a turn near Wormleighton, and this time I wasn't so lucky, only getting round after a great deal of manoeuvering with shaft and engine. Soaked to the skin, I decided to tie up in the middle of nowhere at about half past seven. I had not been along this canal since 1950 when I had been mate on a John Knill boat trading from Middlewich to Reading and Newbury with cargoes of Cheshire salt, but I had a vague recollection that the notorious Griffin's Turn lay between me and 'Finney', and I had no wish to attempt it in the total blackness of a stormy March night.

Having, with some difficulty, put out a couple of ropes, I thankfully sought refuge in my warm, cosy cabin, changing into dry clothes before consuming a substantial and warming meal of tinned steak and kidney pudding and mashed potatoes which had been cooking on the range as I went along. The wind howled and the rain pounded on the cabin roof as I turned in, sitting up in bed for a while to listen to the wireless. When I blew out the light I could see the comforting red glow of the fire, and fell asleep to the sound of storm-whipped wavelets bouncing off the hull.

The storm had abated by morning, but I had a leisurely breakfast, waiting for a watery sun to rise in a grey sky before making a start. When I came to Griffin's Turn I was glad that I had not attempted it in the dark. The bend was acute, the cut changing direction by 180 degrees and, being an inside turn, the towpath was eroded almost to the hedge. I thought of the Skinners and of the two Clayton horse-boats which had been working here only a year previously, and how they had had to cope not only with the mud choked turn but also with an almost total absence of towpath. What heroic struggles must have taken place here, and what anathema must have been pronounced on the management of British Waterways and all its works. Is it fanciful to wonder if the ghosts of frustrated boatmen linger here on dark and stormy nights, their colourful imprecations rivalling the sound of the howling wind?

Beyond 'Finney', which was how boatmen referred to Fenny Compton, lay a stretch known as Tunnel Straight, which had originally been built as a tunnel, but later opened out. The narrow width of this section made it slow going but, once clear of the narrows, there was gloriously deep water all the way to the top of Claydon. Along here I came upon the first of the Oxford Canal drawbridges, enthused over by some for their picturesque appearance, but hated by short handed boatmen. Most of them, this example included, were normally secured in the open position, but enough lowered ones remained to constitute a source of considerable delay. The platforms of these bridges were balanced by two massive wooden beams and, in theory, the method of working them single-handed was straight-forward. The boat was stopped just before the bridge and the boatman went ashore, pushed up the bridge from the 'wrong' side and inserted a suitable stick (a stretcher, which was a length of 3" by 3" used to brace the boat athwart-ships between each beam on a wooden boat, was ideal) to prop it up. He then returned to the boat and drove it through, pulling away the stick as he left the bridge-hole. The platform would then come back down by force of gravity. The trouble was that nearly all these bridges were out of balance, having been pounded by vehicles much heavier than they were designed for, and it often needed Herculean strength to raise them. The one below Banbury Lock needed asistance to raise it even from the 'right' side. Fortunately, though, there were always passers-by here, ready to oblige.

The five locks at Claydon are conveniently close together, so that the boat could be left in one while the boatman ran down to fill the lock below. They were followed by a short and very deep pound separating them from Peter's Three. Then came Cropredy with its wharf and stop place, a pretty little spot, although the pub was a long way from the cut. Here the deep water ended, for a tributary of the River Cherwell crossed the canal on the level, depositing large quantities of silt. The going was slower now, and apart from the shallow nature of the channel, the last three locks before Banbury were widely separated, making it necessary to stop above each in order to fill it.

Below Salmon's Lock, where ranks of loaded iron ore wagons could be seen on the adjacent sidings, waiting to be formed into trains for the long haul to Bilston, Shelton, or over the Stratford & Midland Junction line to

South Wales via Honeybourne, lay the first 'lift-up bridge' needing to be worked. It was right next door to premises known then as Andy's Garage, which was handy as there was often someone about to hold it up for you. Incidentally, I recently came across a photograph of a pair of boats on the Oxford, the motor having had the deck board and mast plank taken down. This would have allowed the fore-end to slide under the platform of lowered drawbridges as far as the mast, enabling the boatman to run forward and prop open the bridge while standing on the boat. This practice obviously saved considerable time, though one imagines that the bridges were better balanced in earlier days.

New Hope's speed had been reduced to a crawl, the Banbury pound being choked with mud, through which loaded boats ploughed rather than swam. After another drawbridge, connecting a meadow with the towpath, I came at last to Banbury. There was a disused basin full of reeds, followed by the boatyard known as Banbury Dock operated single handedly by Herbert Tooley. Alongside lay a half sunken boat, its cabin side still displaying the barely legible name of Hubert Hawkins, once an important Oxford coal merchant.

At this time there were hardly any hire cruisers on the cut, but there were one or two converted narrowboats around. One such lay on the towpath side opposite the dock, a scruffily converted Joey boat rejoicing in the name of *Pookoo*. Nearby were the first working boats I had encountered since Napton Turn, a pair of empty Thos. Clayton tar-boats, captained by Albert Beachy, which did two trips per week between the gasworks at Leamington and the Midland Tar Distillery at Banbury, situated below the lock. Albert's son, Ronnie, lifted up the drawbridge for me and I was soon in Banbury Lock. There were drawbridges above and below the lock, and these were locked at night together with gates which shut off the towpath. The reason for these precautions was to protect the piles of coal on Banbury Wharf which would otherwise have been accessible to light-fingered citizens by walking across the lock gates. Although a number of coal merchants still stored their railborne coal on the wharf, the only boat that unloaded there was Joe Skinner's *Friendship* with its monthly cargo of house coal for Lampreys. Boats were not allowed to tie up for the night at the wharf, though this regulation was sometimes flouted. In a pile of old papers, I discovered a letter in which the Oxford Canal Co. complained bitterly to Thos. Clayton's about the habit of one of their captains, intent no doubt on topping up his coal supply, of mooring at the wharf all night and refusing to move when requested.

Boats were gauged at Banbury Lock and, once this had been done, I struggled through the next drawbridge – the worst on the cut – to find moorings on the towpath side below the lock. It was mid afternoon, and I needed to stop and go shopping. Having done this I was disinclined to start up again, it being a Saturday. So I had a leisurely sit down meal, visited the Public Baths (a feature of every town in those days of many houses without bathrooms) and went to the pictures, finishing up with a pint at "The Struggler" which was the pub used by boat people of whom Banbury boasted quite a few, now retired. In 1879 there had been 74 boats registered here.

I was not entirely alone below the lock, because a pair of John Knill boats lay at the Co-op wharf a little further down, their cargo partly unloaded. From them I heard that John had sold his boats to the Samuel Barlow Coal Co. and had gone to work for them as manager of the boats and dockyard. This was disastrous news. John had been at the forefront of efforts to restore trade to the cut. The Banbury Co-op traffic was one example of a contract regained after being lost to the railway for several years. On the Junction as well, his boats often returned from their journeys to the Colne Valley Sewage Works with cargoes new to the cut, such as timber for Welford on the Leicester Branch and wood wool from West Drayton to Birmingham. He had been trading as a carrier since 1949, starting with a pair of ex Grand Union boats called *Columba* and *Uranus*. His earliest sphere of activity was trading from London to Birmingham, returning with Warwickshire coal to the Home Counties. Short of a full crew for the pair, he then transferred to the North West area, working *Columba* as a single motor. I had joined him at Braunston in January 1950, making my first voyage with a cargo of coal from Baddesley Colliery to Bellis & Morcom's works at Birmingham, before going down the Shroppie to bring a load of salt south from the Cerebos factory at Middlewich to Newbury. It was for these pioneering salt runs, and in particular our epic first trip to Newbury, that John will long be remembered. A detailed account of my adventures with the 'John Knill Navy', as it was affectionately called, is to be found in my earlier book, "Anderton for Orders".

Memories of the salt boats still lingered on the Oxford. "Great big boats they were, use ter come through in the middle of the night," recalled one lock-keeper nostalgically, referring to John's Grand Union steel boats which were bigger than the wooden ones normally used on the Oxford.

Those had been heady days, when enthusiasts were convinced that only a little imagination and enterprise would bring back trade to England's narrow canal system; but despite the bad news regarding John Knill, supporters of water transport were not as discouraged as they might otherwise have been, because of the expanding activities of the new Willow Wren company. John's operations had been squeezed between the low rates needed to recover traffic, and the higher wages needed to attract reliable boatmen, of whom there was a persistent shortage in the South East, dating back to the pre-war years when the Grand Union Canal Carrying Co. had to sell off a number of boats (*New Hope* was one) which it was unable to man. John was not the only small carrier to cease carrying around this time. The Wyvern Shipping Co. of Leighton Buzzard also stopped this activity, though in their case a successful hire boat business was built up instead.

It was with some excitement that I set off on Sunday morning. As far as Banbury I had been working over a waterway which still had some regular traffic, but I had been told that no boats had been beyond Banbury so far that year. Below Banbury Lock stretched a line of wharves and factories. On the towpath side were a mill and a tar works. On the outside, wharves included the Corporation, the Light, the Co-op, Palmer's coal wharf and, next door, the United Dairies factory, another of Joe Skinner's jobs. There were others, long disused. The town is soon left behind, the cut resuming its isolated atmosphere, pursuing its willow and alder fringed course through the Cherwell water meadows. Every now and then there would be a lock, many with no lock house, and those that had a resident lock-keeper were nearly always very out of the way and accessible only by boat or towpath wide enough only for bicycles and horses.

The first road to cross the cut is at Twyford Wharf nearly three miles from Banbury, and this is followed by the isolated Kings Sutton Lock, cut off from the village by the un-bridged Cherwell. I remembered Kings Sutton well, as it was from here that I had been sent by train to Hayes to collect a part for one of John Knill's boat engines. The nearest canal bridge is a good mile from the village and station. Here the railway over the Cotswolds from Cheltenham, which ran through an iron ore district around Bloxham, crossed the cut to join the main line. A little further on at Adderbury was a derelict stone structure that I then thought was a lime kiln, but which Joe Skinner later told me had been an ironworks. I never had time to stop and examine it, but it might have been an early blast furnace.

Below Kings Sutton Lock I was surprised to find the boat shooting forward as the depth of water increased dramatically. This pound, from Kings Sutton to Nell Bridge, was used as a reservoir to supply the Great Western line with water for Aynho troughs. Troughs were laid between the rails in the days of steam engines to enable them to replenish their water supplies at speed by lowering a scoop into the trough. The pound had been dredged accordingly and was so deep that even in a dry spell, when the consumption of water had lowered the level by as much as 18 inches, loaded boats could still navigate. On this March day the Nell Bridge pound was 'running weir' and its length of nearly two miles was covered in short order and at an exhilarating pace, so I was soon rounding the turn by a farmyard to reach Nell Bridge Lock. The A41 bridge immediately below the lock was unusual among those on the Oxford by having no towpath under it, and the parapet sported pulleys and rollers to enable boatmen to get horse-boats under the bridge and into or out of the lock. Imagine motoring along today and coming across a tow-line stretched across the road!

Below Nell Bridge the cut closely parallels the Cherwell, which crosses it on the level half a mile further down, the towpath being carried over it on a series of low arches protected by baulks of timber. This crossing caused considerable delay when the Cherwell flooded because the towpath along this stretch would vanish under water. In February 1950, on the occasion of the first salt run, we had been held up in Banbury by this for several days. Immediately below the crossing is Aynho Weir Lock, of shallow fall and with a diamond shaped chamber designed to allow extra water through with each locking, to compensate for that consumed by the next lock at Somerton which had a very deep fall. The cut became progressively shallower and, after Aynho Wharf – the first convenient tying up place below Banbury – I found myself creeping along, finally coming to a dead stand a quarter of a mile further on. No amount of reversing and taking a run at the scour had any effect, so I had to stay where I was. Fortunately the lock-keeper at Somerton became aware of my plight and contacted the canal inspector at Oxford.

The reason for the scour was not far to seek. A small brook discharged its waters, and any mud they carried, into the canal at this point, and the silt it had brought down had completely blocked the cut. The silting up of canals is often blamed on bank erosion caused by motor boats, which is certainly a major factor, but the mud deposited by river crossings on the level, and by feeder streams without any form of weir to trap the silt, are serious offenders, and one could not help feeling that water supply to the Oxford Canal in the Cherwell Valley might have been better arranged. Having tapped the Cherwell at Cropredy and Aynho it seemed to me that further supplies from assorted muddy brooks were superfluous. Even on regularly used sections of canal, a local cloud-burst could cause a feeder stream to throw a bar across the canal overnight which would stop the first loaded boat. There were also places where the discharge from storm drains and from industrial premises caused heavy silting.

At 9 o'clock on the Monday morning, Mr Aubrey Jones, the inspector for this section of canal, appeared with a borrowed tractor and *New Hope* was heaved with brute force through the scour. I set off once more towards Oxford, but the going was painfully slow. Where silt is allowed to enter a canal, it is pushed along by the passage of boats until the canal is either dredged or a large mileage becomes affected. The next lock, Somerton Deep, was another isolated place, and the people who lived there were glad to have someone to talk to. I lingered over a glass of homemade wine, exchanging some coal for a few new laid eggs and a rabbit which was a welcome addition to the stewpot. They opened the bottom gate for me, which was handy, because if I had been alone I would have to have left the boat to descend in the chamber on its own, having tied the tack string to the arm actuating the gear lever, pulling this to put the engine into gear after I had opened the huge single leaf bottom gate, and stepping aboard as the boat emerged past the lock's tail.

For two dreary miles to Heyford Common Lock, *New Hope* crept along at a snail's pace. Beyond here the depth gradually improved. At Heyford Common began the most entrancing part of the Banbury to Oxford journey: Heyford Mill Lock, remote and tree-shaded, the villages of Upper and Lower Heyford, followed by the lonely reaches beyond. At Heyford Mill there was a new 'lift-up' bridge easily worked, but while I was ashore I became aware of a telltale cloud of steam from the cooling water outlet denoting a blockage. Scrubbing the outside grid with the 'boat's bottom' brush had no effect, so I had to stop the engine, shut the seacock and unscrew the top of the mud box, a square iron box with a filter designed to trap mud drawn into the cooling system. The inside was a solid mass of slimy mud which had to be scooped out with fingers into a bucket. This was the result of my recent muddy adventures and I would have been well advised to have shut the seacock while being pulled through the scour. Once *New Hope* had an airlock in her cooling water system it was often difficult to get it working again, and it gave intermittent trouble all the way down to Three Pigeons where it finally cleared.

Heyford station, right by the cut opposite Heyford Wharf, was the last sign of civilisation for many miles. As the canal pursued its secret course southwards, the water became deep and clear. So clear, that sizeable fish could be seen lurking under the bank as I went along. Kingfishers darted about, flashes of blue against the black hedges. Another isolated lock, Dashwood's, was followed by an equally lonely one at Northbrook. This was marvellous boating; the sort of thing I had often dreamed of during my enforced Egyptian exile, and could only have been improved by meeting another boat now and then. Five years prior to this a dozen boat-loads of coal reached Oxford in an average fortnight, and ten boat-loads of tar a fortnight came up from Oxford to Banbury in addition to the occasional salt boat. In February 1950 I had been among five loaded boats tied up together at Enslow. Now, alas, I had the cut below Banbury all to myself.

Before long I was floating by the site of the long disused quarry and cement works near Kirtlington, now a magical carpet of rabbit nibbled turf and wild flowers broken by romantic ruins. Many people, of whom I am one, find great satisfaction in the abandoned relics of mining and industry. Certainly, when recovered by nature, they are often picturesque. Will our descendants find the remains of Heathrow Airport or Spaghetti Junction so intriguing when their time comes, as come it surely will? The pyramids, the Roman roads, the Great Central main line; all massive artefacts whose makers envisaged that they would remain in use for ever; all now mere ruins to while away the time and tempt the imagination of the curious.

These works, belonging to the Oxford Cement Co., were opened in 1906/7, and depended entirely on canal transport as they had no rail or road access. Many Number Ones worked to the Oxford Cement and it had been Joe Skinner's first job as a young owner boatman. Coal was brought here from various collieries, the furthest away being Cannock, Baddesley and Measham on the Ashby Canal. In 1922 they produced 17,287 tons of cement, about fourteen boat-loads a week, despatched by canal to various destinations, much of it being transferred to the G.W.R. at Bletchington station, where the mooring rings can be seen to this day in the stonework abutting the site of the goods yard.

Judging from the amount of correspondence in the Oxford Canal papers, the Oxford Cement Co. must have been regarded as an important customer. It was noticeable that there was an unusually large amount of concrete work on the canal in these parts, including the coping of locksides above the top gates and the edgings of some wharves. One concludes that the canal company may have carried out repairs and additions with the locally obtained concrete rather than with brick or stone. Generally little concrete work was to be found on the narrow canal system at that time, except for the extensive bank protection work in the 1930s on the Grand Union Canal with the use of concrete piling and capping.

Half a mile below the works lay "The Three Pigeons" pub, alone on its island between the canal and the Cherwell and reachable only by a cart track. This was a boatman's pub and, like Aynho, one of the regular tying up places; although Enslow, just over a mile further on, was equally convenient. Here there were two wharves, a coal wharf on the outside above the bridge and a roadstone wharf beyond on the towpath side.

Below Enslow I came to Gibraltar Lock where the canal entered the Cherwell and used its course for nearly a mile. On my first trip down the Oxford in February 1950, the Cherwell had been in flood so that the towpath was under water and boats were delayed. A loaded boat was an unwieldy animal and it was with some trepidation that I locked out at Gibraltar into the fast flowing current, for it had rained heavily when I crossed the Northamptonshire uplands where Cherwell's waters had their source. The river twisted and wound through meadows and rushy banks and *New Hope* sped down the reach at a brisk rate. Between Gibraltar Lock and the railway stood the new cement works that had been built to replace the old one at Kirtlington, though this time there was no connection with the canal, the works being served by a siding from the Great Western main line. John Knill had hoped to bring coal to the works, unloading above Gibraltar Lock and getting the coal into the works on a short tramway along the towpath. He had also attempted to re-start the once substantial roadstone traffic to wharves at Cropredy, Banbury, Heyford, Enslow and Kidlington, and was able to quote a competitive rate. Unfortunately British Waterways insisted on charging a high rent for the use of the former roadstone wharves which, at that time had been long disused and had, then, no prospect of anyone wanting to rent them. Not surprisingly the project fell through.

After about ten minutes spent on the river, I spied a wood on the outside bank, and knew that the exit back into the cut at Weir Lock was close. The gate was open (the lock was supposed to be left ready for downhill boats) and I steered into the narrow entrance, being unable to reduce speed because of the need to maintain steerage way when making the turn across the current, so as to avoid being carried on down the river sideways. Fortunately there was a bar of mud across the entrance, sufficient, even with the water level being about nine inches higher than usual, to slow me down as I entered the lock, so I was able to 'bring-up' without undue difficulty.

Like the lock below the river crossing at Aynho, Weir Lock had a shallow drop and a diamond shaped chamber. Below it lay one of the Oxford's most enchanting reaches – a mile of deep, reed fringed water. Skirting Shipton, with its church reflected in the canal, I came upon Thrupp wide, a great pool of water lilies. I was tempted to linger in this delightful setting, but the reality of boating life abruptly intruded at the far end of the wide, in the shape of Thrupp Turn, a right-angled bend whose concrete edging bore the marks of more than one encounter with an iron stembar. Dick Littlemore, born and bred on the Oxford Canal, told me not long before he retired that even he 'missed' the turn about once every ten trips. To complicate matters, the turn was spanned by a drawbridge. Beyond this bridge lay a straight length lined with the cottages of Thrupp village, home of the Beauchamp family of former Number Ones.

Thrupp marked the end of the deep countryside through which I had wended my way from Banbury. The rapidly shallowing cut, having passed under the main road bridge, proceeded to skirt the fringe of Kidlington, with its roadstone wharf and the older Langford Lane Wharf which was the maintenance depot for this section. I would have liked to have stopped for the night at Thrupp and enjoyed a chat with the retired boatmen who frequented "The Britannia", but having had so much delay I felt obliged to press on. However, I didn't get far, for by half past seven I was firmly aground on a scour at the bottom of Round Ham Lock, a mile below Thrupp.

At eight on Tuesday morning the maintenance gang flushed me off the scour, and I made the remaining six miles to Oxford in two and a half hours. There were only three more locks to deal with – Kidlington Green, Dukes and Wolvercote – and two drawbridges. Below Dukes Lock I passed the narrow arm which led to the Thames. It disappeared beneath a roving bridge and passed through a stop lock equipped with four gates to allow for fluctuations in water level on the river. This Dukes Cut Branch ran for six furlongs to join a backwater of the Thames above Kings Weir. Boats for Wolvercote Mill, which had stopped receiving coal by water in 1951, turned off this branch after a quarter of a mile, winded, and dropped backwards down the mill stream to reach the unloading wharf. Latterly the traffic had been handled by S.E. Barlow of Tamworth, but at one time the mill had its own boats, having purchased two in 1856 and sold them – though presumably not the same craft – in 1916. In 1884 the cost of transporting coal the 107 miles from Moira was 13/3 ½ d per ton, in 1897, 14/5d. The mill was consuming about 100 tons per week in that year. At one time the Oxford Canal Company had its own wharf at Eynsham on the Upper Thames, but the last coal was delivered to it in 1925. I became friendly with the lock-keeper at Dukes and would often linger over a chat and a cup of tea in his tree shaded garden.

Suburbia closed in after Wolvercote Lock, and I began to pass the large houses of North Oxford with their gardens coming down to the water.

Here and there were large coal wharves, reflecting the ability of the relatively well off academics to keep their houses well heated. Throughout the 19th century Oxford was regarded as one of the plums in the domestic coal trade, and heated battles were fought by various interests to get a share of it. In those days Warwickshire coal was in competition with coal mined in the Forest of Dean and brought to Oxford through the Stroudwater and Thames & Severn canals, and the Upper Thames; and also with the Somersetshire collieries whose coal reached the city by means of the Kennet & Avon and Wilts & Berks canals. A fascinating description of these battles for 'market share' is to be found in that excellent book, "The Oxford Canal", by Hugh Compton.

The number of factories on the canal in Oxford was small, the most important being the Radiator Works. The last half mile of the canal into the city was dreary and badly silted. It was sad that the final approach by canal to Matthew Arnold's city of dreaming spires was not much better than a miserable ditch. All the houses, wharves and factories were on the outside of the cut, the towpath being separated from Port Meadow and the Thames only by the railway. It was pleasantly tree-shaded and a haunt of the local girls and American servicemen who had an apparently insatiable desire for intimate contact with each other.

CHAPTER TEN

SPRING ON
THE OXFORD

•

At 10.30 a.m. I tied up at Juxon Street Wharf and unloading began immediately. The arrangement at Oxford was that four members of the maintenance gang would be sent to unload a boat, being paid 5/- each. The coal was unloaded with a shovel and wheelbarrow and stored on the wharf, being collected by Morrells Brewery as required. While this was being done I went shopping and had a walk round town.

There was, of course, no back loading available. Time was when the Oxford Canal traders had returned to the coalfield with cargoes of round timber, hay or straw. In those days the builders, not only of canal boats but also of railway and road wagons, used quantities of oak and elm, whilst the once numerous dray horses, boat horses and pit ponies had to be fed and bedded. With the demise of the working horse these traffics had disappeared. Mary Prior, in her book "Fisher Row", gives an interesting account of how loads were obtained by the owner boatmen in days gone by. Fisher Row was a street of cottages fronting one of the Thames backwaters in Oxford, and the home of many of the old families of Oxford watermen.

However, I did make a few enquiries about possible back loads, going to see a Mr Hull, transport manager for the Radiator Works, as it was known, although other motor vehicle components were made there as well. He seemed interested, telling me that the works had only stopped having coal by canal because the poor quality of coal available immediately after the war had compelled a change to fuel oil; apparently, amongst other things, the coal dust had got into the machinery. So perhaps had Warwickshire coal been washed, as was the case with most of the South Staffs pits, this contract might have survived a few years longer. We discussed the possibility of transporting the firm's products to the car assembly plants of the Midlands, but the problem was that, in order to reduce the cost of financing inventories, vehicle assemblers now expected to receive parts "before they were made". Another possibility was the removal of scrap from the works, but this idea too came to nothing.

From time to time other suggestions for back loading off the Oxford were mooted. For instance, the carriage of Thames Valley gravel, loaded at Langford Lane Wharf, to Coventry and the carriage of aluminium from the factory at Banbury to Warwick and King's Norton. I also made enquiries about more coal traffic, going to visit Hall's Brewery in Oxford. This seemed promising at first, but fell down on the objection that their coal came from Kingsbury Colliery which was not canal connected, and being satisfied with the quality of coal, they did not wish to change. Certainly there could, and should, have been more traffic on the southern part of the Oxford Canal. For instance, Banbury iron ore was sent by rail to blast furnaces at Bilston and Shelton, both on the cut, and these works could also have received scrap.

A lot of the trouble was that the canal carrying industry lacked vigorous and able entrepreneurs. The only person in the long distance trades who could be so described was Leslie Morton, manager of the Willow Wren Company and a founder manager of the Grand Union Canal Carrying Company in its expansionist days of the 1930s. But Willow Wren had only just started up and was preoccupied with its business on the Grand Union, although it was later to enter the Oxford trade. John Knill was already out of the game, and S.E. Barlow approaching retirement. The Samuel Barlow Coal Co. were not interested in chasing new traffic on the Oxford because of the generally bad condition of this canal and the susceptibility of traffic to interruption by flood or ice. They preferred their boats to race up and down 'The Junction', doing a trip in a week with a full load and making them money. British Waterways drew its management from the old Grand Union company and were firmly orientated towards the traditional traffic pattern of coal to the Home Counties and imported goods back from London Docks. They had, however, inherited a small amount of timber traffic to Banbury from Fellows, Morton & Clayton, who they had taken over in 1949, so the blue and yellow livery was to be seen on the Oxford Canal but only very occasionally. Incidentally, Samuel Barlow still had a contract at the time to Sandford Mill on the Thames in Oxford, but they had been carrying it by lorry for some years and would not consider putting it back on the cut.

Another problem in the South East was the difficulty in recruiting and retaining boatmen. This was nothing new, the Grand Union company had experienced the same problem before the war. The 1950s was a period of very high employment, with the booming car manufacturing industry pushing up wage rates rapidly. The carrying companies had always relied upon the sons and daughters of boatmen to take up the same occupation, but now they had to try and recruit labour 'off the bank'. Where they could crew pairs of boats with families this was successful, although obviously very few people wanted to bring their families up on canal boats. One would have thought that the freedom of boating life would have appealed to single men, even if they could only stick it for a few years; but such all male crews that the carriers obtained would leave after a few trips. The reason lay in the way the work was organised. Carrying companies only employed the captain who was in turn responsible for providing and paying his crew. There were ample opportunities for crews to fall out amongst themselves, quarrelling over who should steer the motor and who the butty, blaming one another for going aground and other mishaps, arguing about what hours to work and when and where to tie up for the night. The rigid insistence of the South Eastern carriers for working boats in pairs, which was not relaxed for several years, meant that when one member of a crew left, the other then had to give up the boats as well. Contrast this position with the North West, where there were not only pairs of boats, but motor boats working singly crewed by only one man. There was, at this time, always a waiting list for such jobs, being ideal for the adventurously minded young man who was not yet ready to settle down.

The situation was not much better with the few all male crews composed of born and bred boatmen. Most of them changed their composition with bewildering rapidity and they were also prone to change their employers at frequent intervals. There were a few exceptions: Ted Barratt junior worked with his brother Ken for several years, as did Alf Townsend and his son. The Townsends, who hailed from Abingdon on the River Thames, were former Number Ones.

Ironically, there came a period in the late 1960s, when it became fashionable to 'drop-out' of conventional society. Then it was that many people sought to take up the boating life but, alas, that way of life no longer existed in the way it had still done a decade earlier. To all intents and purposes canal transport was finished, and the more determined 'drop-outs' had to make do with ploughing a lonely furrow along canals otherwise deserted by trade, retailing coal from their boats. This was not even a shadow of the real boating experience in the days when there was still a community of several hundred boats at work.

When the last of the coal was out, I swept up the hold (always known as the boat's 'bottom') and gave *New Hope* a thorough mopping off. I had had ample time to clean the engine room, cabin and outside brasses so all was smart and clean for the return journey. A pot of potatoes sat on the range ready to be moved onto the hotplate to boil, and a piece of steak reposed in the oven. At four o'clock I untied and went down below Louse Lock to wind. There is nowhere on the canal itself at Oxford where a full length boat can be turned, the terminal basin, half a mile further on from Juxon Street, having been sold and filled in. Here there were once extensive wharves and a warehouse spanning an arm of the canal. Back in the 1830s, Oxford had been served by seven fly-boats a week conveying goods from London, the Midlands and the North. These were operated by the firms of Pickford and Crowley. There were also two market-boats and three other services to and from Banbury. Canal-borne goods were received and forwarded by barge and road between Oxford and Southampton, Portsmouth, the Isle of Wight, Reading and Newbury. In competition with the fly-boats for London traffic, four sailings a week were offered to the capital via the Thames. At one time the canal wharves at Oxford were accessible not only to narrow boats, but also to Thames barges of which the canal company owned several, so there must at one time have been a wide lock connecting the two waterways.

Louse Lock (its proper name was Isis Lock) always gave the impression of being tiny, in fact the first time I saw it I could hardly believe it was big enough to take a full sized boat. This was an illusion, for naturally it conformed to standard canal dimensions, though there was only a small difference in level. Below the lock there was a three-way junction of Thames backwaters, and I winded the boat by turning the fore-end upstream and then dropping back astern, before going ahead to re-enter the lock. The journey back up the cut with an empty boat was peaceful and easy and I was tied up at Thrupp by half past seven with my dinner cooked and ready to dish up. After a leisurely meal I washed up and repaired to "The Britannia" where, as I expected, I fell in with several old boat people.

From Thrupp I went to Finney and from there to Sutton's where, as there were no orders for Oxford and as I had business in Birmingham, I decided to go down to Pooley and put in a load for the G.E.C. My log records that "extreme difficulty" was experienced with this trip. After unloading I stayed the rest of the day at Salford Bridge, celebrating the first anniversary of my demob day.

On enquiry I found that the Boat Control office at Sutton's had slipped up, forgetting that there was now a regular boat on the Morrells' job, and had allowed a consignment of coal to go by rail. I therefore decided that on my way back to the coalfield I would stop at Ted Jones's yard and have the engine overhauled after its hard winter's work. Events overtook me however, for I had got no further than 'The Bakehouse' when I broke down with clutch trouble and had to be towed to Glascote by an Element's horse. Leaving *New Hope* at Ted's, I continued on to Pooley where I picked up a loaded Joey boat and came back to Kettlebrook, proceeding to Birmingham the next day.

What had happened was that two brass dogs in the clutch had become badly worn. This was caused by the weight of the reverse lever resting on them in forward gear. The lever extended up to the engine hole roof, its top end being connected with a rod which ran back to the steering position. The trouble was simply cured by fixing a collar on the reverse rod to limit its forward travel. It took nearly a week for the spare parts to come from Ruston's factory in Lincoln, but I was conveniently placed to catch the early bus each morning to Salford Bridge and to do a bit of work for Elements who, as usual, were short of boatmen. They had resorted to getting S.E. Barlow's Joey boatmen, Franky Woodhouse and his son of the same name, to work some boats from Pooley as far as "The Beehive" at Bodymoor Heath, whence they were taken forward by Element's own boatmen. The Woodhouses were paid a pound a trip for doing this, and young Frank described it as "the most miserable job we've ever had."

Ted Jones had been an engineer on sea going ships before swallowing the anchor and starting up his own business at the former Samuel Barlow Coal Co. dock at Glascote. Ted and I often enjoyed an hour or two of argument over politics and current affairs in his cosy bungalow on the dock and, if I should happen to be there at a weekend, Mrs Jones would always cook me a tasty Sunday dinner. He was a very clever man when it came to things mechanical. An inventor of some note, he was never stuck for a solution to an awkward engineering problem. One interesting job done at his yard the previous year was the conversion of the narrowboat *Bath* from screw propulsion to a form of jet propulsion. The original National engine had been removed and two 9 h.p. Coventry Climax engines installed. Water was drawn in through holes cut in the hull alongside the engine hole, and this fed two horizontal Hotchkiss Cone propellors. It was expected that the boat could be steered by varying the speed of these propellors separately. However, on trials with an experienced boatman at the helm, the system was found to work well enough on the straight, but *Bath* could not be steered round the sharp turns in the Atherstone Pound. The boat belonged to John Knill's brother-in-law who traded as the Coronet Canal Carrying Company. The experiment having failed, he was forced to sell *Bath* and her butty *Matilda* to Samuel Barlows, who re-converted her to screw propulsion. To the best of my recollection,

Coronet never actually carried any cargo. The failure of this experiment was a disappointment. Had the difficulty of steering been overcome, it would have solved the problem which was causing an enormous amount of trouble on some canals, of conventional propellors being fouled with rubbish or weed. Perhaps, had it been possible to pursue this experiment further, success might have been achieved, as I believe that Hotchkiss Cones were successfully fitted to a narrowboat converted to pleasure use only a few years later, the ordinary rudder, in this case, being retained.

When the engine was ready I went to Pooley for a load to Coventry Light and then resumed the Oxford run. This time the trip was free of trouble. After completing loading at Griff I went to Stretton, and from there to Finney; the third night saw me at Aynho and the fourth at Oxford. The round trip took seven days without a break except for the time spent loading and unloading. On the third trip to Oxford I had an extra cargo, five pipes from Hillmorton to Langford Lane, for which I was paid four shillings.

It was now well into April and springtime spread its mantle over the countryside. The towpath hedges turned from black to a delicate shade of green and the first primroses appeared. I had always enjoyed being out and about in the dark, so that when there was a delay in unloading on my fifth trip, I decided, having spent the previous two days doing nothing, to work all night. Stopping off at Thrupp for a pint, I emerged into the delight of a scented May night. There was a full moon and scarcely a cloud obscured the stars piercing the black canopy overhead. Hour after hour, *New Hope* slipped unobtrusively through the sleeping countryside, her passage marked only by the subdued splashing of her wake on the margin. In the long straight above Dashwood's the moonlight made a path on the water, shivered into fragments by *New Hope*'s fore-end, churned by her wash, but resuming its unbroken gleam as the ripples died away. With the engine quietly ticking over while the lonely locks – Dashwood's, Northbrook, Heyford Common – were filling, the hoot of owls could clearly be heard. Away over towards Steeple Aston a fox barked briefly and unseen creatures rustled in the undergrowth.

There is no experience to compare with working a canal boat in the dark on a fine night. You are alone with no one to observe your secret passage through town or countryside. Familiar landmarks look different and there is the extra thrill of overcoming navigational difficulties in the dark. Lock after brick dripping lock was left behind as I worked steadily up the Cherwell Valley, a mug of tea on the cabin top, the warmth of the fire and the cosy lamplit cabin below my feet. I had no headlamp, nor did I need one on a night so clear as this. It was 2.30 a.m. when I arrived at Banbury and there I was forced to tie up, the lock being closed for the night. I slept for a few hours, an eight o'clock start being early enough to take me to Newbold, only three hours empty boating away from Sutton's.

On arrival I reported to the Boat Control office, and being unable to load at Griff before the weekend, received orders for Pooley instead. Going down Atherstone Locks, I was working in the usual way, that is, leaving the boat to drop down in one lock while running down to prepare the one below, when one of those mishaps inseparable from boating life happened. On returning to the boat in the second lock, I discovered a jet of water from the top gate pouring straight into the cabin. Everything was soaked, including a loaf of bread which I had bought at the top lock and left lying on the side bed. Hastily refilling the lock, I pulled *New Hope* back above the top lock. Although quite a bit of water had entered the cabin, it had not caused the bilgewater to come over the floor, which was lucky as the bilge was oily. But the bilge had to be pumped out – with the hand-pump as the water was up to the flywheel in the engine hole – and the cabin had to be thoroughly dried and cleaned. What had happened was that an obstruction had lodged between the gate and the cill which, as the lock emptied, caused water to leak into the chamber under pressure. The cabin doors had been left open so there was nothing to stop the water going into the cabin.

From then on I was very careful to close the cabin doors and pull the slide across when leaving the unattended boat descending in a lock. This being done, the gate could leak as much as it liked without any ill effect. By the time order had been restored I didn't feel like starting up again and going down the locks, so I stayed at the top of Atherstone and went to the pictures. Next morning I went down to Pooley, and after emptying at Coventry Light, set off again for Griff.

When I got to Bedworth Hill, which was a popular tying up place with a pub called "The Boat" opposite the Newdegate Arm, who should I find tied up there but my old friend Ray White with the *Thomas*. Tying up alongside, I was entertained to tea in *Thomas*'s cabin while Ray poured out a tale of woe. The contract for the supply of coal from Cannock to Townsend's Mill at Worcester had been terminated. Having no other work for it, Charlie Ballinger had sold *Thomas* for conversion into a house-boat at Braunston, to where Ray was now taking her on her last voyage behind a horse. Ray had been promised a pair of Barlows when he got there.

Back in 1952, Ray was the boatman mentioned in the first chapter who was sacked from Barlows for colliding with one of their crack captains while navigating Braunston Tunnel by the light of a candle in a jam jar. That had been in the days of Le Cheminan, but there was now a new king in Egypt, John Knill, now being Barlow's fleet manager. Ironically, as related in "Anderton for Orders", Ray had also once been sacked by John Knill. The wheel had turned full circle: 'Chemmy' had gone, John Knill no longer owned any boats, but Ray was still pursuing a successful boating career. After his death in 1987, an obituary notice remembered him as a man who "loaded them deep and worked them fast."

We visited the stable so that I could pay my last respects to Bob whose career as a boat-horse was now presumably at an end, and who would be ignominiously returned to his owners, British Railways, from Braunston station in a horse-box. Would he, I wondered, miss the excitement of the hurley-burley of boating and his boat-horse companions of many a night in the stables at Worcester, the Bar Lock and Walsall Wood?

So passed away the last Severner horse-boat and now only Joe Skinner worked a long distance boat by animal traction. Over a pint of beer in "The Boat" that night, Ray and I concocted a valedictory poem the flavour of which can be conveyed in the following extract:

"Last of the Severners, withdrawn from trade,
Awaits at Braunston its unholy fate.
No more for slack boats Townsend's Mill shall wait
The memory of their passing soon shall fade.

No more the furious strife, the voices shrill
Of swearwords whistling round the horse's head.
The Cut is dying, and will soon be dead;
The last boat waits its turn for Wainlode's Hill.

But when the moon shines full on Tar'bigge spire
They say that the Last Severner sails again,
A ghostly longboat, gliding down the lane
Of moonlight twixt the segs. Ere they retire
Men lock their doors and as they cower in fright
They hear the tumult of its passing by;
The dread voice of its Captain and the cry:
"Draw up! Draw up! The Cut is open all night!"

In the morning Ray carried on to Braunston, where he was to take over *Tiger* and *Jane*, and I went into Griff for Morrells.

As week followed week, and spring ripened into summer, I became absorbed in the world of the Oxford Cut. I was keeping the job going comfortably and did not always bother to hurry. A few buckets of coal to barter with kept me supplied with eggs and vegetables. Rabbits were now out of season, but often I would tie up for the night in some remote place and put out a night line for eels with which both the canal and Cherwell abounded. I would linger to exchange the latest gossip with lock-keepers; commiserating over a glass of homemade wine with an indignant or resigned account of some wayward daughter's pregnancy; listening with astonishment while mothers, and sometimes even grandmothers, speculated on the physical attributes of the black American servicemen who were stationed at several bases around Oxford, the nearest to the cut being at Upper Heyford whose deafening aircraft often roared over the canal. In an age when many country people had still travelled little further than the nearest market town, and when rural isolation was a real fact of life, they evinced a great curiosity about foreigners in general and negroes in particular, but simply could not understand, when it was explained to them, the segregational policy of the American Forces. To them it was as outlandish a conception as making gypsies or Irishmen – or even boat people! – use a separate pub from the locals.

Sometimes I would spend a night at Oxford, tying just above Louse Lock and having a wander round the city followed by a modest pub crawl. The main boatman's pub in Oxford was the "Nag's Head" and one could still meet retired boatmen in the bar, together with a sprinkling of well off undergraduates and Yankee servicemen. I soon learned that you could be treated to many a pint in exchange for boating reminiscences, though in order to indulge in this game it was necessary to dress in something resembling the popular conception of boating attire rather than my usual conventional going ashore gear. A good deal more boating was done in the "Nag's Head" than ever happened on the actual cut, and boatman vied with boatman to invent the most lurid tales of fires in tunnels, multiple drownings and bodies chopped up in the blades or kicked to death by horses. The art of story telling still lived!

A lot of boatmen – for it had been only a few years previously when there was still a brisk trade here – knew their way well around Oxford and could tell you all about the different pubs, but I was a stranger. One night, quite by chance, I went into a pub opposite the gaol. I ordered my pint and stood at the bar drinking it when, on surveying the room, I became aware that the clientel was composed almost entirely of brightly dressed and heavily made-up women. I drowned my drink and was making ready to leave when one of these ladies accosted me. "Don't go yet," she said,

"Have a drink with me." Embarrassed, I politely excused myself and left, not giving any further thought to the matter until, some time later, I happened to mention it to a boatman who was well acquainted with Oxford. "Don't you know," he laughed, "That's where all the prossies hang out." But to this day I have not worked out why one of those ladies wanted to buy *me* a drink. The walk back along the towpath from Hythe Bridge to the boat had to be made carefully for fear of tripping over horizontal courting couples who, on a warm summer night, seemed to cover every spare foot of grass.

June brought the famous 1955 strike of railway footplatemen. Great Britain still depended very heavily on rail transport and people brought up in today's environment, where most goods travel by road, will probably find it difficult to conceive what a serious matter this was. Coal merchants who were supplied by rail, but who still had canalside wharves, immediately went running, cap in hand, to the carriers. In most cases, though, they were disappointed, as there was little spare capacity even in the summer. The first effect of the strike on me was felt on my arrival at 'Sutton's' on the 9th of June where, on going to the Boat Control Office, I was surprised to be ordered to Newdigate to load for Banbury.

Newdigate was an arm off the Coventry Canal at Bedworth Hill, served by a colliery railway from the pit which was on the outskirts of the town. The track from the arm, by which you could walk up to the main road, rejoiced in the name of Black Bank. Boats here were loaded in exactly the same way as at Griff; in other words the coal was shovelled out of railway wagons to the accompaniment of clouds of black dust. It was a busier loading place than Griff and the coal was of better quality, though not as good as that from Baddesley. My cargo was of household coal and came in large lumps which shook the boat alarmingly as they tumbled into the hold.

The consignee was a firm called Palmers whose premises were at Cherwell Wharf below Banbury Lock, a little further down than the Co-op wharf. They were already a customer of S.E. Barlow in so much as they were the factors for the coal supply to the United Dairy at Banbury. However they did not normally receive their domestic coal by canal, though substantial stocks were kept on their wharf. Anyone canvassing these canalside coal merchants met with the same answer. The platform of a delivery lorry was at the same level as the floor of a railway wagon, enabling the bags to be filled while on the lorry. With a canal boat, coal was first shovelled (and usually barrowed as well) on to the wharf, then the bags had to be filled on the ground and man-handled on to the platform of the lorry for delivery. At this time even the simplest mechanical aids

"This looks like ours!"

Summer on the Oxford.

were almost non-existent in the domestic coal trade. But what of the stocks held on the wharf? It was still thought to be cheaper to shovel coal from railway wagon to lorry, carry it to the wharf which was usually close by (less than a quarter of a mile away, at Banbury) and then shovel it out into a pile on the wharf, rather than incur the cost of shovelling and barrowing out of a boat. There could not, I thought, have been much in it; the rate paid for shovelling and barrowing from a boat being usually 3/6d per ton at this time in this area. On the other hand, the men and lorries used to transfer coal for stock between station and wharf would only represent a marginal cost as they would normally be employed on retail deliveries. Putting coal to stock would only be a small proportion of the total through-put, much of which was done in the summer months when the demand for retail deliveries was at its lowest.

Readers may be curious as to why the adjacent Banbury Co-op was receiving regular supplies of domestic coal by canal. The inclusive rate for tolls, carriage and unloading from Baddesley to Banbury Co-op was 19/6d per ton. That from Newdigate to Palmers, a journey 11 miles (or nearly 20%) shorter was 21/-. So the Co-op coal was being carried at rather a tight rate. The United Dairy, which was next door to Cherwell Wharf, was a different matter. Here the coal was thrown directly into the boiler room and, had it been brought from the station by road, it would have been barrowed off the lorry. The cost advantage here was firmly in favour of the canal.

By the time I got loaded it was too late to bother to go any further than Sutton's that night. The next day's journey to Marston Doles took rather longer than usual as, both the fifteen mile pound between Hillmorton and Napton, and some of the pounds up Napton locks, were low. but there was adequate water in the summit and I reached Banbury the following evening.

At Palmers I found I had to unload the 22 tons 10 cwt cargo myself, the coal having to be barrowed to a pile well back from the waterside. I had done quite a lot of shovelling coal into boats, but that was downhill work and took only a couple of hours. Discharging a boatload of coal by hand is not exactly heavy work, in fact, if there were two or three of you it was not much more than healthy exercise lasting only a few hours. Single-handed, it was another matter. It was very much slower, having filled each barrow I had to climb out of the boat to empty it, and of course it was extremely boring and tedious. Making stops for tea and snacks resulted in coal dust being trampled onto the counter and into the cabin. Single-handed, it was just about possible to barrow out a load of coal in a working day, but only by working unremittingly. The one advantage of barrowing was that there was none of the effort required to fling the coal back as far as possible or throw it on to the top of a mountain of coal which might already be occupying a too small wharf, something which had to be done in many places. Instead, you were only lifting each shovelful about five feet from the floor to the barrow.

I had tied up above Banbury Lock the previous night, so by the time I had got up rather late, had breakfast and negotiated the two drawbridges and the lock, it was ten o'clock before I started shovelling. As usual I had left a break to the floor behind the mast, so that there was not much coal to get out of the way before I could start shovelling on the floor. With small coal you could start shovelling off the top of the cargo, but a shovel would not dig into large lumps, needing rather to be slid beneath them.

I set to with a will, and after about an hour a sizeable mound of coal had grown on the wharf but – and this was the infuriating thing about emptying – the amount in the boat seemed hardly diminished. There were some enormous lumps in the cargo and these had to be lifted out, picked up and carried to the stockpile, and arranged in a wall which served to contain the smaller pieces. Hernias caused by lifting these huge lumps without breaking them up were not uncommon among the older boatmen. As the pile grew higher, a plank was laid up it, the barrow being pushed up the plank so as to raise the height of the pile and prevent it from taking up too much room on the ground; for, of course, the wharf was covered with piles of various grades and sizes of coal.

At about half past eleven, Ronnie Beachey appeared on the wharf. He was the teenage son of Albert and Sue Beachey who worked a pair of Claytons carrying tar from Leamington to Banbury, where they discharged at at Midland Tar Distillers. While some people, including myself, were not terribly keen on shovelling coal, for many boatmen it was a sought after activity as it was paid at a higher rate than actual boating. So, if there were any boatmen around when a boat was unloading, offers of help were usually forthcoming. In fact, it was not uncommon for a boatman who was actually travelling, to tie up if he encountered someone that he knew who would welcome assistance. For young Ronnie, the 25/- he got for helping me get out the rest of the coal was a useful and welcome amount of money.

I made a pot of tea and then we got stuck into the coal, using two barrows and taking it in turns to fill and wheel. At one we knocked off for fish and chips and a pint of beer. Little by little the amount of coal in the boat shrank, the floor being swept up to the remaining piles as we went along.

By eight in the evening it was all out, the beams and planks replaced, and everything mopped off; but it was just too late to lock up and tie up above the lock for the night.

S.E. Barlow had asked me to canvas Palmers to see if they would give us some more loads but none materialised; though they did, in the course of the discussion, show me their railway rates. In any case, Morrells needed another load, and it was while I was on my way down to Oxford with this that I was accosted by Welford's agent at Aynho Wharf. Welford's were a big firm of Banbury coal merchants and Aynho was one of their depots.

"Mr Welford said, would you bring him a load of coal when you get back," the agent shouted across to me. I had some time previously canvassed this very agent only to be met with the usual explanation about higher handling costs by canal compared with rail. Now he was begging for a boat load! I rang up S.E. Barlow, but all the boats were fully employed and, by the time I got back to the coalfield, the railway strike was over. A pity, as I would have liked to deliver a load of coal to Aynho Wharf right under the nose of the Western Region station master.

Some readers may well be asking why British Waterways did not lower their tolls to attract more traffic. In fact, it was possible to negotiate special tolls below the standard rate: but as long as there was one traffic between two places paying the full toll then they would not reduce on other traffics between the same two points. The standard toll on coal to both Banbury and Oxford was 6/- per ton. The argument was that they would have had to reduce on existing as well as new traffic. Furthermore, the shortage of crews in the South East meant that resources devoted to carrying new traffics would almost certainly be abstracted from those engaged on existing and more profitable cargoes.

With the end of the railway strike the temporary additional demands for canal transport ceased. The drivers and firemen had won a much deserved increase in wages, but at the cost of alienating a Conservative Government who, already influenced by the powerful road lobby, decided to give more encouragement (at the taxpayers' expense) to road transport. They felt that the Unions were less capable of organising the road workers, but that they were well capable, as had just be shown, of organising the rail unions into disruption of the economy. Within three years a friend of mine would take me to view the construction works of the M1 motorway; within twenty-five the entire country would have been transformed into a motorised hell.

Fortunately, Providence has arranged that we cannot see the future, so no such horrid visions were able to intrude as I ambled through the as yet undisturbed countryside between Coventry and Oxford. To those of us whose business was on inland waterways, it seemed inconceivable that the trade should ever cease. Small carriers might go out of business, a few outlying sections of canal might lose their trade, but to imagine that the great canalside power stations served by fleets of boats should ever close, that the paddles on 'The Junction' might one day fall silent, or the water of the Wyrley & Essington become deserted and weedy, was wholly beyond our imagination. Were not British Waterways, Barlows and Elements still launching new boats, and would they be doing so if there was any prospect of a total collapse of trade?

Since I had stepped down from the train at Braunston on that April day in 1954 I had rarely been away from the environment of the cut, but on arrival at Oxford that weekend I decided, being a devotee of Matthew Arnold, to make a pilgrimage to the countryside so vividly evoked in "Thyrsis" and "The Scholar Gypsy". From Abingdon to Newbridge the Thames makes a great loop of twenty-three miles, to connect two places which are only six and a half miles apart as the crow flies. Within this loop lie the Cumnor Hills, a low wooded range rising to around 500 feet. Armed with my much thumbed copy of Arnold, I caught the bus to Hinksey and sought "the track by Childsworth Farm", its hedges festooned by dog roses and its verges heavy with creamy white flowers of cow parsley. I climbed up past the wood to the top of the ridge. Southwards lay the long whaleback of the Berkshire Downs, whose secret byways I had explored so avidly in my schooldays, their bare heights dividing Thames from Kennet. Turning, I gazed westwards, where, against the dim blue backdrop of the Cotswolds lay "the Vale, the three lone weirs, the youthful Thames." Bees hummed among the harebells and, in the distance, a branch line train, trailing its snowy plume of steam across the landscape, whistled for Witney station, its haunting sound drifting up to me across the valley. Finally I looked towards the east where Oxford, Arnold's city of "dreaming spires" which, in the words of the poem, "needs not June for beauty's heightening," spread her towers and steeples out below me.

Finding a sunny spot, I reclined on a bed of springy, rabbit bitten turf and read again the legend of the Scholar Gypsy who, three hundred years before, had deserted Oxford's halls of learning to wander the countryside in the company of gypsies, seeking what we would nowadays call the secret of transcendentalism. Just as he had rejected the conventional life of his day, so too had I; abandoning comfortable suburbia for the hard, yet infinitely more satisfying life of a canal boatman. My mind went back over the events of the last year: the high hopes as I had prepared *New Hope* at

Braunston, so soon to be dashed by the disasters which had followed; the almost miraculous, it sometimes seemed to me, recovery of my fortunes. I thought of all my experiences: of working on the last horse-boat to Worcester, of discovering the intricacies of Joey boating, of new cuts explored and old haunts revisited. With my boat in good shape, and confident of an ongoing canal trade, I felt I could look forward to many more years of this agreeable way of life.

Rising at last, I sought my way, surrounded by all the sounds and scents of a summer afternoon, down the hill towards the inn at Bablock Hythe, my thoughts turning in the direction of a foaming pint of beer to be enjoyed by a foaming weir. From there I would take the Thames towpath to Eynsham and catch the last train of the evening – a steam train, how could it ever be anything else? – back to Oxford and my waiting boat.

GLOSSARY

Backering Where a horse pulls a boat without having anyone on the tow-path to drive him.

Big Engine Motor boat fitted with 15 h.p. Bolinder engine.

Beams Four removable lengths of wood about 6 inches wide and 2 inches thick placed athwart a boat's hold.

Block Rope Extension of tow line used in conjunction with a pulley block to give extra purchase when starting a loaded horse boat out of a lock.

Boat-snapper Man employed to move unattended boats around at a loading or unloading place.

Bracing Chains Chains attached to each side of the hold of a boat under each beam and connected by a bottle screw. The chains were undone while loading so as not to obstruct the hold, and tightened up to pull the boat's sides into the beam at other times. Joey boats did not have bracing chains, the beams being permanently fixed in place.

Cabin Boat Canal boat fitted with residential accommodation and registered as a dwelling.

Company's Men British Waterways maintenance workers

Cross-wind To allow a boat to enter a lock or narrow place at an angle thus bringing it to a stop and possibly doing some damage.

District (the) Archaic boatman's term for Birmingham and the Black Country. Old documents often describe this area as "the mining and manufacturing district".

"Draw Up!"	Command given by captain to open a paddle.
Edgeford Arm	Hednesford Arm, the boatman's name for the Cannock Extension Canal. In Black Country parlance, "ednes" was corrupted to "edge", e.g. Wednesbury being pronounced as "Wedgebury".
Fast	Aground.
Formaldehyde Boat	Open iron horse boat fitted with cylindrical tanks. These boats traded from Ryder's Green to the British Cyanide works on the Smethwick feeder branch of the Titford Canal. They also formerly traded to Tyseley. The cargo had to be delivered without delay, otherwise it would solidify in the tanks.
Ganzy	Rushall Canal
Hobbler	Man informally employed by boatmen to help them through a lock flight.
Inside	Towing path side of the canal.
Joey Boat	Type of boat used for short distance work around Birmingham and the Black Country. Lighter in construction than a cabin boat and with no residential accommodation, though a small cabin for shelter was often provided. Also known as an Open Boat.
Knobstick	A boat belonging to the Anderton Company
Looby	Spring loaded peg on mast, arranged to automatically release the tow-line if fouled.
Number One	An owner boatman.
Oil Rod	Control used to vary the speed of a Bolinder engine.
Paddle	Apparatus for letting water into or out of a lock.
Peg To	To attach the towing line to the mast.
Port Claytons	Thomas Clayton boats engaged in carrying oil between Ellesmere Port and the Black Country.
Pup	9 h.p. Bolinder engine.

Room	The hold of a boat was divided into four sections known as rooms: fore-end, back of the mast, stern middle and back end. In the Severn area rooms were known as quarters and some Severner boats were divided into five quarters! Each room was separated from the next by a beam and, in most wooden cabin boats, the rooms were subdivided by removeable stretchers.
Segs	Boatman's name for sedges or rushes.
Steerer	A contractor providing labour and towage to work boats belonging to other firms.
Stretcher	Removeable piece of 3 x 3 inches timber fitted athwartships in the middle of each room (except the fore-end room) in a wooden cabin boat.
Standed Boat	An unattended boat left for loading or unloading at customers premises.
Stemmed Up	To go aground.
Tat	Valuable scrap.
Top Bend	Uppermost plank in the bow of a wooden boat which was made to assume two curves, inward and upward, and also with a degree of tumble-home.
Wind (to)	To turn a boat.
Winding Hole	Wide place in canal for turning boats.
Windlass	Detachable handle for operating paddles.